Praise for *Do You Know Who I AM?*

"Angela tells God's truth in a world that desperately needs divine direction. This book will change your life!"

—Karen Kingsbury, America's No. 1 inspirational novelist and author of the *New York Times* bestselling Above the Line series and *Unlocked*

"Biblical, real, funny, witty, and life changing. Angela understands a woman's heart and offers God's path to freedom through addressing 'brave questions.'"

—Julie Clinton, President, Extraordinary Women

"Thank you, Angela, for taking on tough issues women face with sound, biblical teaching. May God continue to guide you as you meet women where they are through your powerful gift of encouragement and unique ability to equip them."

—Pam Case, Director, LifeWay Women

"The title of this book alone penetrates the deepest places in our hearts. *Does God know me? But how do I know?* Angela walks us through the questions all of us ask ourselves at one time or another, the kinds of thoughts we're too embarrassed to say out loud. Our character is flawed and yet God's is perfect. *Is He sure He wants to use me?* Be ready to be comforted, to be encouraged, to be strengthened, and to fall into the arms of the Great I Am who gives us more than hope. The real question is: *Do I know who God is?* No matter where we are in our journey with Christ, self doubt always has a way of entering in. Be reminded of who you are in God's eyes and who God is in your life."

—Candace Cameron Bure, Actress

DO YOU KNOW WHO I AM?

AND OTHER BRAVE QUESTIONS WOMEN ASK

ANGELA THOMAS

HOWARD BOOKS
A DIVISION OF SIMON & SCHUSTER, INC.
New York · Nashville · London · Toronto · Sydney

Howard Books
A Division of Simon & Schuster, Inc.
1230 Avenue of the Americas
New York, NY 10020

First Howard Books trade paperback edition October 2010

HOWARD and colophon are trademarks of Simon & Schuster, Inc.

For information about special discounts for bulk purchases, please contact Simon & Schuster Special Sales at 1-866-506-1949 or business@simonandschuster.com

The Simon & Schuster Speakers Bureau can bring authors to your live event. For more information or to book an event contact the Simon & Schuster Speakers Bureau at 1-866-248-3049 or visit our website at www.simonspeakers.com.

Designed by Renato Stanisic

Manufactured in the United States of America

10 9 8 7 6 5 4

Library of Congress Cataloging-in-Publication Data

Thomas, Angela
  Do you know who I am? / Angela Thomas.
    p. cm.
  Includes bibliographical references.
  1. Christian women—Religious life. I. Title.
  BV4527.T4675 2010
  248.8'43—dc22   2010012408

ISBN 978-1-4391-6070-1
ISBN 978-1-4391-7759-4 (ebook)

FOR SCOTT
YOU ARE A GIFT TO THE CHILDREN AND TO ME.
GOD KNEW EXACTLY WHAT WE NEEDED WHEN HE GAVE YOU TO US.
I LOVE HIM SO MUCH FOR THAT.
WHAT A JOY TO CALL YOU MY HUSBAND AND MY FRIEND.
I LOVE YOU LIKE CRAZY.

CONTENTS

FOREWORD

Paul ran and finished hard races. When I think of a person who embodied courage, determination, and spiritual stamina, Paul of Tarsus is my guy. And it seems he always arrived at the finish line composed and breathing evenly. From a distance, his life looks all put together . . . but that is at the finish line.

A closer look reveals that Paul often started his races in the men's room, green around the gills, overcome with anxiety, and painfully aware of his shortcomings.

Paul's trip down memory lane recounting his early church-planting days in Corinth reveals how aware he was of his weaknesses. He wrote, "When I came to you I didn't come presenting the Gospel with polish or pizzazz, and I didn't wow anyone with my words of wisdom. . . . I was scared. I couldn't stop shaking."

So what changed Paul from the guy hurling in the bathroom before the race to the calm, collected figure we see standing on the awards platform?

In this book, Angela reveals the truth about where real courage, determination, and spiritual strength are found.

She describes what many aren't saying these days . . . we *don't* have what it takes. Unless we connect with the One who meets us when we get real with Him about our weaknesses.

Do You Know Who I Am? will encourage you to rethink your fears and limitations. Angela will help you discover that when you stop pretending you have it all together, God then reveals who He is, in and through your weakness.

I have known Angela for years. I have seen her exit some bathrooms on race day looking green around the gills. She still occasionally trembles. But she runs. She lives what she writes about. She has found that God breathes His life into her life, especially where she declares her need for Him. What she writes about she lives.

Read this book . . . even if your hands are shaking. You'll be glad you did.

Brad Brinson, Sr, Pastor
Two Rivers Church, Knoxville
Pastor to Angela

INTRODUCTION

My friends Jessica Wolstenholm and Kathy Helmers brought the title of this book to me. And honestly, I really didn't like the idea at all. *Do You Know Who I Am?* It seemed so self-centered and pointless. Whom could I ask? My friends? My husband? My kids? No one can really *know* me, right? They know parts of me and they have impressions of me, but the idea of writing a book about wanting to be more known made me feel sad. No one feels truly known. Nope, I had another book in mind. One that wasn't depressing and defeated.

About six months passed, and I prepared to write the other book. But one early morning, between 4:30 and 5:00, God woke me up. Just waking up in the middle of the night never happens to me, because I am great at staying asleep. No dreaming. No list making. At bedtime, my mind turns off and goes to sleep, sometimes before I actually lay my head on the pillow. That particular morning, I woke up in the dark thinking, *This has something to do with God.*

Later, I was sure it was God because the very first thought that came to me was, *"The question is for Me."*

Huh? My mind wasn't processing. *What does that mean, "The question is for Me"?*

And then I heard, *"You are supposed to ask the question to Me. No one else can give you the answer except Me."*

I was sitting up on the side of my bed, making notes, at this point. *What? God wants me to ask Him, "Do You know who I am?"* Then it finally struck me, *That's exactly who I'm supposed to ask. No one can know me like God. But what about all of my weakness? All of my struggles?* Then I realized that's what I'm supposed to ask God about. My needs. My flaws. The insecurities. Struggles. Pain. All of it. The questions are for God.

And so, that morning, I began to make a list. I was writing so fast and furious that my hand couldn't keep up with my head. *God, do You know that I am tired? I feel inadequate. I want to be a better mom and a better wife. I am insecure. I feel defeated. I get my feelings hurt.* Everything just poured out of me. At the end of my searching, I had written more than a hundred struggles, needs, weak places, and insecurities. I didn't even know what to call them; I just knew that what I had been keeping inside now had permission to come out. Each thought I offered to God as a question and a prayer: *Do You know this about me? Do You see this? What about this part of me I never talk about?* The morning was spent in pure, gut-wrenching honesty before Him.

But here is the most amazing thing. I had spent more than an hour searching my soul with questions for God. And when I didn't have any more questions to ask, God spoke into my spirit with a question for me. "Angela, do you know who I AM?"

When I didn't have any more questions to ask, God spoke into my spirit with a question for me.

I don't know how else to describe it, but immediately, there was a complete and settling peace in my soul. And then there was joy, such a beautiful, quiet joy. God's response gave the deepest kind of soul stillness. The questions stopped. The personal struggle ceased. The answer had been given. The answer is knowing God. Knowing God! That is always the answer. Who He Is. The answer to my need is always found in God. In His character. In His being. My questions that morning had taken me to God. Hallelujah.

And so this book began with my questions, but it has become about the character of God. What I want to tell you is this: I am only beginning to know God. Every page of this writing has clearly shown me how very little I know, and all the study of these months has made me long to know Him more.

As I began writing, I took my list of a hundred needs and struggles and whittled it down to twelve. Only twelve. Good grief, that seems so few. I tried to start with the honest questions and stories that might be attached to your heart and life as well. Then I asked God, *Do You know who I am?* With every chapter, I searched for the character of God, His heart toward us. I wanted to know Him more.

Here is the thing. I can never write enough to do justice to the character of God. I can't study enough or be smart enough. His attributes are as vast as His being. His character is both known and a mystery. Nothing I have written could even begin to encompass who God is. These chapters are just a beginning—a human effort to know the eternal God of the universe, a God who is not too big to know you and me. I pray this book moves you toward who God really is in your everyday life. I am hoping you will grow accustomed to taking your questions to God. I pray that your search for answers will always take you to His character and His Word.

And I pray that something inside these pages, by the power of the Holy Spirit, will cause you to want to know God more. He is the answer. His Word is our guide. His character meets every need. His goodness is perfect. His love is everlasting. His mercy is new. His justice is merciful. His presence is more powerful than we know. My friend, more than I can ever say in measly, limited words, I want you to know the God who is I AM.

As I have been writing these past months, I have been reading some great books I'd highly recommend, so that you can know God more.

Knowing God, by J. I. Packer.
The God of All Comfort, by Hannah Whitall Smith
The Knowledge of the Holy, by A. W. Tozer
Your God Is Too Small, by J. B. Phillips

J. I. Packer wrote these profound words that helped shape my heart toward this work:

What matters supremely, therefore, is not, in the last analysis, the fact that I know God, but the larger fact which underlies it—the fact that *he knows me*. I am graven on the palms of his hands. I am never out of his mind. All my knowledge of him depends on his sustained initiative in knowing me. I know him because he first knew me, and continues to know me. He knows me as a friend, one who loves me; and there is no moment when his eye is off me, or his attention distracted from me, and no moment, therefore, when his care falters.

This is momentous knowledge. There is unspeakable comfort . . . in knowing that God is constantly taking knowledge of me in love and watching over me for my good. There is tremendous relief in knowing that his love to me is utterly realistic, based at every point on prior knowledge of the worst about me, so that no discovery now can disillusion him about me, in the way I am so often disillusioned about myself, and quench his determination to bless me.

There is . . . great incentive to worship and love God in the thought that, for some unfathomable reason, he wants me as his friend, and desires to be my friend, and has given his Son to die for me in order to realize this purpose.[1]

And, as with all the writing I have ever done, I am so very humbled that you would spend your time with my words. It is a privilege to share my stories and my studies with you. Every day I have said to the Lord, *I want to know You more.*

May it be the same for you.

You are worthy, our Lord and God, to receive glory
and honor and power, for you created all things,
and by your will they were created and have their being.
—REVELATION 4:11

CHAPTER ONE

Do You Know
I Am Afraid to
Dream Big?

He Is Worthy

Last week I went to London and Paris.

Before you get carried away with dreamy visions of romance and strolling violinists, let me explain. Last week I went to Europe with my daughter Taylor and thirty other students and chaperones from her school. All very great people. An itinerary that would make you drool. But, alas, it was January.

I travel all the time, mostly around this country, but several times a year internationally. And it is no exaggeration for me to tell you that those eight days in Europe were, hands down, the most difficult travel of my entire life.

Sure, we started well, giddy at the airport, packed for cold weather, and armed with umbrellas, French dictionaries, and a good dose of "can do" spirit. We dreamed of hot tea and scones, Trafalgar Square, the Palace of Versailles, and chocolate crepes. *Merveilleux!*

But did I tell you that it was January? Did I mention the hostel outside London with the cross-dressing party in the lobby? Make that the freezing-cold hostel, two subway rides from the city. It was the craziest kind of trip, where the subways were randomly closed and we just walked and walked and walked . . . in the cold and rain . . . everywhere. Most days we were away from our rooms about fourteen hours. Everyone was completely exhausted and trying desperately to hang on to an adventurer spirit. But the truth of it was, most every day was hard.

But all the days together could not compare to last Tuesday.

Last Tuesday we departed our hotel around eight in the morning. The first two subway rides were frustrated by the same trouble we had every day. Each trip, one of our kids would be stuck on the other side of a turnstile with a ticket that wouldn't let him through. There were several again that morning. But finally, we were there. The Louvre Museum. And that day we had come to see the *Mona Lisa*! Our group huddled outside the Louvre in umbrella-breaking wind, waiting for the tour guide to return with our tickets. We couldn't wait to be inside, wandering around in the warmth, staring at the great works that awaited. At last our tour guide returned. *Closed*. I am not kidding, the Louvre was closed. But only on Tuesdays in December and January.

Our dreams were squashed. But it was just a couple of subway rides over to the Champs-Élysée—a beautiful outdoor boulevard lined with upscale shopping. At the end of this amazing place is the Arch of Triumph, a must-see, even in the bitter weather. So I rustled up my pack of kids, we pulled our hoods tight, and using umbrellas to shield us from the incoming rain, we forged into the wind and made a path toward the arch. The rain was blinding by the time we reached this famous landmark. I yelled to my kids, "Caannn yoouuu seeee it?"

Through chattering teeth they replied, "Yesss."

"Taaake a picturrrre," I said. Click. Click. We turned our backs to the wind. Umbrellas down. We ducked into the nearest bistro for hot chocolate until it was time for the next assignment from our tour guide.

Next stop, the Eiffel Tower. By the time we got there it was raining, spitting snow, and the wind was blowing at what was later reported to be hurricane force. At the bottom of the tower, there were only a few other tourists and us. Finally being there was nothing like you dream it will be. No strolling musicians. No hot crepes.

No souvenir stand to buy berets. Nothing. The Parisians were all inside like sane people should be.

I know you may think I am exaggerating, but we have the video to prove it. The kids looked like reporters from the Weather Channel, standing in front of the fog-soaked tower, holding onto anything for dear life, while the unrelenting winds threatened to lift them off their feet. Now this is the craziest part: in that kind of weather, the Eiffel Tower was still open. Not the very top, hallelujah, but high enough—two elevator stops up.

I thought, *There is no way we are going up in this thing. It can't be safe to be any higher in these winds. Surely we should just go find somewhere warm and dry.* But high school hearts prevailed and you guessed it, we loaded up all those kids for an elevator ride up the Eiffel Tower. Taylor turned away from the window and buried her head in my coat. "Mom, this is more like the tower of terror," she said with a laugh.

At the second stop, we were all blown out through the open doors, laughing and half-crying over the awful weather and our plight. There we were, standing around the edge of the Eiffel Tower looking out into the fog, scared of the swaying signs, frozen by the wind and snowy rain, wondering what in the world we had done. It was awful and exhilarating at the same time. Thank goodness for the tiny gift shop way up there in the sky. We all piled in and bought little Eiffel Tower key chains, ran to the outside concession stand for more hot chocolate, and just plain huddled together until it was time to leave.

The trip down the elevator and the walk back to the subway were the rotten chocolate on the frozen crepe. More scary wind and freezing rain. By the time we got on the train, everyone was soaked to the bone through their coats and shoes. Drenched, crazy,

> *It was awful and exhilarating at the same time.*

exhausted Americans. As we rode along underneath Paris, the adults looked at one another and began to ask, "Why in the world did we just do that?" Good grief, it was kind of dumb, and yet, we had plowed along, taking those kids up in the Eiffel Tower.

Eventually we decided why we had persevered. One of the teachers said it first. For most of the thirty-two on our trip, this would be the only time they would ever see Paris, and today was the only day in a lifetime they would ever visit the Eiffel Tower. And in just a moment, we didn't feel dumb anymore. We felt like conquerors. Soaked and weary and victorious. Today, if you asked those kids what their favorite memory of our trip was, every one of them would tell you, "The night we almost died on the Eiffel Tower."

That night, back in my warm Parisian bed, I basked in the understanding that the whole wet, tiring day was worth it. It was once in a lifetime for most of us. One opportunity to see the Eiffel Tower and one trip to pack in as many memories as we could. One dream come true. Then I realized the same is true in our relationship with God. We have one lifetime. One short amount of time to do all that He has intended for us to do. One heart to surrender. One passionate mission. One offering of all that I am.

Maybe you hear yourself say to God, "Do You know that I'm afraid to dream big? Do you know that I'm scared of swaying Eiffel Towers? And walking through storms? And commitment to things that are bigger than me?" The truth is, on my own, I might have gone to Paris and stayed in my room that stormy day, missing everything. I probably would have settled for a warm bath and snuggled up with a book. And there, very safe and dry in my hotel room, I would have missed the once-in-a-lifetime adventure and the victory of a dream fulfilled.

Here is the thing I never want to forget. With this one lifetime, I am called to follow Jesus. No hesitation. No holding back. I am called to follow Him with everything my personality and mind can give to Him. To be a passionate woman who runs hard after God.

I am called to dream big. And so are you.

Here is the reason: Our God is worthy.

I AM Your God Who Is Worthy

I'm sure you know firsthand that this world is a dream stealer. Just about the time you decide to head for the Eiffel Tower dream in your life, hurricane-force storms blow through to discourage your plans. The weary heart and the exhausted body can decide to play it safe. Your head might reason, "Turn around and go home. It's too dark out here. This journey is too hard. What if something goes terribly wrong?"

I guess I've used that argument a million times or more. Little gusts of difficulty and gale-force winds of rejection have turned me back time and again. But I am learning, in these middle years, that God does not intend our lives to unwind and taper off. We have been given one lifetime, and He purposes that we keep growing, keep improving, keep building His kingdom, and keep dreaming of how we might make His glory known.

We are supposed to persevere. Struggle on. Climb the mountain. Follow through. Carry on. Go the distance. Run the race. It's just that sometimes I forget why. Mostly I forget who God is. And frequently, I forget who I am in Him.

In the book of Revelation, John writes, "You are worthy, our Lord and God, to receive glory and honor and power, for you created all things, and by your will they were created and have their being" (Revelation 4:11). Because we are created by God and because we have our being in Him, He is worthy of our worship. Worthy to have our lives bring glory to Him. Worthy of every honor each day can bestow upon Him. Worthy of powerful work and love done in His name. The message of Scripture is loud—do you hear it? God is worthy. There are two parts to this declaration:

God does not intend our lives to unwind and taper off.

One—God's very nature is worthy of all glory and honor and power.

Two—You and I are called to live every single day with God's character in view.

We have each been given a tremendous opportunity with this gift from God called a lifetime. With our lives, we are called to bring Him all glory and honor and praise.

Why should we dream big dreams for our lives? *Because God is worthy.*

Why should we keep trying to become more mature followers of Christ? *Because God is worthy.*

Why should a woman work really hard to keep a healthy soul? And dream of a healthy marriage? And long for a healthy home? *Because God is worthy.*

Why should we choose to live meaningful, compassionate, other-centered lives, giving our talents and our love away? *Because God is worthy.*

We are called to follow Jesus Christ and dream big dreams in His name. *Because God is worthy. God is worthy. God is worthy.*

Until we stand in eternity with our Lord, our *calling* means that we do what has been entrusted to us and that we do it for Him. Paul wrote to the Ephesians: "I urge you to live a life worthy of the calling you have received" (4:1). I love the beautiful paraphrase of *The Message*: "I want you to get out there and walk—better yet, run!—on the road God called you to travel. I don't want any of you sitting around on your hands. I don't want anyone strolling off, down some path that goes nowhere."

Because He is worthy, we are supposed to live worthy. This calling means spending the rest of our lives seeking to know God, purposing to learn His truth through Scripture, and then living like we remember who God is.

No strolling off down some path that goes nowhere!

Therefore

In the first three chapters of Ephesians, Paul writes about the blessings of being a child of God. These chapters contain doctrines of our faith, outlining all that we, as believers, have received from God's goodness. But Paul makes a turn at chapter 4. In the first verse he writes: "As a prisoner for the Lord, *then*, I urge you to live a life worthy of the calling you have received."

Most theologians agree that here, the word *then* would be better translated as *therefore*. Essentially, Paul is saying, "Therefore, go

live a life worthy of everything
I just taught you about God."
Being worthy is God's nature.
Living worthy is our calling.

Being *worthy is God's nature.*
Living *worthy is our calling.*

The first three chapters of Ephesians are packed full of God's gifts to us. Look at what you have received:

- God has provided you with every spiritual blessing. (1:3)
- You were chosen by God for God. (1:4)
- Your life is redeemed and your sins are forgiven. (1:7)
- You are sealed by the Holy Spirit. (1:13–14)
- God gives you a glorious inheritance and His incomparably great power. (1:18–19)
- You are made alive in Christ. (2:5)
- By grace you are saved. It has nothing to do with your works. (2:8)
- God prepared good works for you to do. (2:10)
- You are not far away from God anymore. (2:13)
- Christ is your peace. (2:14)
- You have access to the Father by the Spirit. (2:18)
- You have union with other believers. (2:19)
- You are indwelt by the Spirit. (2:22)
- You are an heir to the promises of Christ Jesus. (3:6)
- You can approach God with freedom and confidence. (3:12)
- You can be filled to the measure of all fullness. (3:19)
- God is able to do more than all you ask or imagine. (3:20)

I don't know if you just zipped through that list or if you lingered, but either way, I urge you to go back and reread the list of gifts God promises to you. Maybe it would mean more to insert your name before you read each promise.

Can you believe God? How good He is to us. His gifts to us are wonderful and extravagant. I hope that brief list made you pause. I hope your spirit was reminded of who God is. I hope you remembered that God is worthy of a life well lived. A big life, with big dreams.

In the book to the Ephesians, and right now, today, Paul writes across our lives, "Therefore." He says, You have been given much and God is so worthy, *therefore,* go live a great big life worthy of your calling in Christ Jesus.

Our calling is not supposed to be restrained or squandered or hidden. God calls us to so much more. He wants us to live like He is worthy.

Multiply Your Talents

Jesus uses a parable in the book of Matthew to explain what God desires of us. It's called the Parable of the Talents (Matthew 25:14–30). Before we jump into the Scripture, I have to tell you that just rereading this story has moved me to tears. Personal, deep tears. Today, I am truly writing to you from my own longing and the truth I know. Everything in me wants all that God has for me. I want to live fully devoted to Him, faithful to take risks for His name and ready to step out in faith wherever He calls. I want to dream big all the time. I want to pursue my own personal growth and dream big for my husband, my children, and my ministry.

But fear has always been my enemy.

Studying this parable today reminds me afresh that fear can keep me from dreaming in multiples for God. And He is so very worthy of my gifts being multiplied for His glory.

Fear was the enemy in Jesus' story too. The parable goes something like this:

There was a master with three servants. The master was going away for a very long time, so he gave each one of his servants some of his property. To the first one he gave five talents (a very large sum of money), to the second one he gave two talents, and to the last servant he gave one talent. Each was entrusted with an amount according to his abilities. And then the master left.

The first two servants doubled the master's money while he was away. The third one dug a hole and carefully buried his master's property.

After a long time away, the master returned and called his servants in to settle up with them. The first two servants were able to tell the master they had doubled his investment. And to those two, the master said, "Well done, good and faithful servant! You have been faithful with a few things; I will put you in charge of many things." (Matthew 25:21, 23)

Next it was the hole digger's turn, the servant who had buried the one talent that was given to him. The servant said to his master, "I was afraid I might disappoint you, so I found a good hiding place and secured your money. Here it is, safe and sound down to the last cent" (verse 25, Message). The master was furious with the last servant and said to him,

> That's a terrible way to live! It's criminal to live cautiously like that! If you knew I was after the best, why did you do less than the least? The least you could have done would have been to invest the sum with the bankers, where at least I would have gotten a little interest. Take the [talent] and give it to the one who risked the most. And get rid of this "play-it-safe" who won't go out on a limb. Throw him out into utter darkness.
>
> —Verses 26–30 (Message)

The words of the master to the third servant ring loud in my heart. *Living cautiously, playing it safe, afraid to go out on a limb.* I think my tears came because I long to live worthy of everything God has invested in me. Our beautiful Lord deserves multiplied talent, multiplied blessing, and multiplied glory. Oh, merciful Father, please forgive this play-it-safe girl. I want to be more.

> When *the master* leaves a *servant* in charge during his absence, he does not expect to find him waiting at the door when he returns, but rather getting on with the job entrusted to him. . . . [We are] not to be in passive waiting but in getting on with the job and making the most of the opportunities entrusted to us.[1]

Did you hear in the parable that the master gave talents according to each one's abilities? Whew. God gives us talents, but we are all given different amounts according to God's knowledge of our potential. I am not called to multiply your talents in my life. And bless God, you are not called to multiply my talents in yours. We are responsible only for the talents God has given to us.

Tell me, how many times unfair comparison has kept us from living worthy of God's calling? You can look across the room and see a woman with an entirely different set of talents, and yet unfairly compare yourself to her. It's a lose-lose every time. The comparison can leave you doubting yourself. *Maybe God didn't really call you to dream anything remotely big.* And the lies from the comparison win, and we head to the backyard to dig a hole big enough to hide what God has given to us.

Did you also see how sneaky the enemy is in this story? As my kids would say, fear is a "creeper." Lurking. Whispering. Ever-present until we choose to reject its presence and believe God instead. Fear kept the third servant from multiplying his talent for the master. I kind of get it, don't you? The servant said, "I was afraid I might disappoint you, so I went out and hid the talent in the ground."

The pain of remembering what it feels like to disappoint someone we care about can keep us from trying again. I have been paralyzed with the fear of failure and have let opportunities to bless God pass me by. Haven't you suffered an anxiety that kept you from persevering? Caused you to give up? Or made you think that you couldn't? That's what fear does; it tells us to settle for nothing even when God's glory is on the line.

> *Fear tells us to settle for nothing even when God's glory is on the line.*

The servant reported that instead of multiplying his possession, he had just kept the talent safe, but that was not the master's intent. God wants the glory from your talents and mine.

The Faithful One Is Worthy

The man was a corporate big shot.

Actually, he was bigger than a big shot. He was president and CEO of a worldwide conglomerate, and all the big shots worked for him. Year after year he led his business with a focused determination to succeed at every level and expected that same focus from his employees. And they did succeed. High expectations coupled with a driving spirit produced big results. Financial gain, expansion, innovation. He spent a lifetime striving for the victory he enjoyed. Some would have called him a genius.

This very successful man spent the last two weeks of his life in a hospital outside of New York City. And for those two weeks, the only person who came to see him was his wife, who kept a loving vigil day and night beside his bed. No cards or flowers came. No one else called. No priest or pastor. Nothing.

In his final days, he said to a nurse, "I spent my life building one of the largest businesses in the world with over twenty-five thousand employees. But at the end, the only one who is faithful is the woman I have ignored for fifty years."

Oh, the ache of such a misspent life.

I believe that at the end we will stand before the One who is faithful. The one true God. The Everlasting Father. The Prince of Peace. We will stand before the One who entrusted us with talents and every day of our lives graciously and mercifully called us to live for His glory.

The question, for each one of us, begs to be asked: "Will I live a life worthy of my calling, or will I ignore the One who is faithful?"

Paul wrote these words to the church of Corinth, and he also wrote them for you and me: "God, who has called you into fellowship with his Son Jesus Christ our Lord, is faithful (1 Corinthians 1:9).

Our Lord is faithful. Faithfully calling us to rearrange our lives around Him. Faithfully entrusting each one of us with different talents. Faithfully letting us begin over and over again.

A Woman Like Me, a Woman Like You

Somewhere along the way, we got it into our heads that God calls only the perfect or the educated or the successful. Or maybe He gives talents to the young, the healthy, and the happily married.

Somehow we have believed that only the *worthy* can bring glory to a God who is worthy. Turns out that God uses the broken and the lost and the wounded.

This past weekend I met a man in Los Angeles who had lived for years as a homeless alcoholic. He would beg for food or money on the streets around the church that I was attending. Some people from the church began to pay attention to this man. They told him about the unchanging love of God. They introduced him to the Savior he had needed all of his life. They drove him to a recovery program and encouraged him toward commitment. Now, twelve years later, the man came walking along the sidewalk, an integral part of this church body. Sober for more than ten years, working at a good job in the community, and engaged to be married! Wow, what a beautiful sight he was. And what a wonderful God we have. Faithful to keep calling the ones He loves toward His will for their lives.

I meet women all the time who can't believe God is calling them to something bigger. So hear me, for goodness' sakes, yes, God is calling even you to dream *big*! You may know my story: seminary graduate, divorced, remarried mom with four kids. No one anywhere would have ever chosen me to teach the Bible to anyone; well, maybe they would have let me speak at the prison ministry. Some ministries do amazing work all around the world, but because of my divorce, I would not even be allowed to be a discussion leader at their meetings. So go figure, me, a Bible teacher. Unbelievable to some, but God had a beautiful plan for me. I love saying, "But God."

So maybe you are a woman who has suffered many failures. Maybe the scars you bear have made you feel like an outcast. Or maybe you are the church lady who can't believe God would call a woman like you to more than the casserole ministry. I am here to personally testify. God loves to show off His glory wrapped around broken women like you and like me.

So perk up your ears and listen. The deep, abiding love of God is calling you to Himself. He wants you to bring every gift you have to the altar where He is worthy.

Here we are with only one lifetime to serve a loving and faithful God. My prayer is that you will not ignore His call. I pray that your response to His goodness will be an extravagant offering of your gratefulness. That your dreams will be big and that you will push fear aside so that you can put all your weight into the strong arms of

> *God loves to show off His glory wrapped around broken women like you and like me.*

faith. I pray that you will understand what has been given to you in Christ Jesus so that living a "life worthy of the calling" will become your greatest passion.

Tonight, from the comfort of my home, I am remembering our night at the Eiffel Tower. The winds were howling and the rain was a bitter, piercing cold. We couldn't get warm enough and the soaking wet coats and shoes made the day turn to miserable for all of us. No sane person had come to the tower that stormy afternoon, just our group with one opportunity in a lifetime to see its fogged-in majesty. Standing underneath the lattice of riveted iron, I remember how looking up into its eighty-one stories made me feel small and weak. And the winds made me feel hesitant and afraid. To this day, I am amazed that we got into the elevators and rode up anyway. Tonight, as I remember, it seems like we were brave.

In the chair across the room from me is the little Eiffel Tower pillow I bought in the gift shop. It's a peaceful souvenir that completely misrepresents the swaying monstrosity where I bought it. But it makes me remember what doing something big feels like. And truly, for my God who is worthy, that's how I want to live. I want to spend this lifetime learning how to be courageous. Living a bigger story than the one I can write. Dreaming bigger than my mind can imagine. And in the end bringing a greater glory for my God who is worthy.

———————————— ❦ ————————————

Does your heart cry out,
"God, do You know I am afraid to dream big?"
Then listen as God replies to your hesitant heart:

DO YOU KNOW WHO I AM? . . .
I AM your God who is worthy.

The heavens declare My glory. The skies show My handiwork. I AM
the Lord of lords, your great God who is mighty and awesome. I AM
the greatness and the power and the glory and the majesty and the
splendor, for everything in heaven and earth is Mine.

Give your heart to My Son, Jesus, who is the reflection of My glory
and the exact imprint of My very being, who is now sitting at the right
hand of My Majesty on High.

You are My beloved, and I AM your God who is worthy.
Forever and ever, amen. [2]

*She gave this name to the L*ORD *who spoke to her:*
"You are the God who sees me," for she said,
"I have now seen the One who sees me."
—GENESIS 25:13

CHAPTER TWO

DO YOU KNOW
I AM INVISIBLE?

He Is My God Who Sees

Our family just moved to a great Southern town.
Everything is new to us. Church. School. The grocery stores. Soccer. Everywhere we go, we are learning how to navigate being unknown, introducing ourselves, sitting politely while everyone else connects with their friends, and then going back the next time and doing it all over again. Each one of us is waiting patiently for the spark. Something kindred. Some God moment where there is a connection at the heart. We are waiting to be seen.

I have given all my kids great inspirational talks about our adventure. The people we will meet. The ideas we will learn. About going boldly into the unknown and looking for God's path and His provision. They have been amazing in this new town. For weeks, I have watched each one of them walk into rooms of complete strangers only to come out of youth group or their assigned class with a new friend. I've been so proud of my brave kids. Not one whiner among them.

It was just a soccer game and I was sure I could do that. We've probably been to at least a hundred soccer games as a family, so this soccer mom felt pretty confident that particular Monday afternoon. Besides, we had already been to at least four games with this new team, said hello, and yelled alongside them. The soccer game was definitely a no-brainer.

AnnaGrace and I just happened to be the first spectators that afternoon. As veteran soccer watchers, we did what we always do, grabbed the soccer chairs and a few water bottles and made our way over to midfield. We set our chairs up about four feet away from the boundary line and settled in. AnnaGrace did homework, and I watched the boys begin their warm-ups.

After a while, the other families began to arrive. Some time passed, and by the start of the game, I realized no one had come to sit anywhere near AnnaGrace and me. Finally, I turned around and saw that every other family from our team was sitting about ten feet behind us. All in a row with their soccer chairs. All talking among themselves. No one even looked toward us. Not one hello. I instantly felt stupid.

Every other family from our team was sitting about ten feet behind us. No one even looked toward us. I instantly felt stupid.

I began asking myself, "Are we sitting in the wrong place? Did I miss some kind of memo about where to put my chair? Have I done anything to any of these people I don't even know? Why does this feel so goofy?"

Almost as quickly, I began considering all the other games I'd been to. "This is where the parents have always sat, so maybe they don't put their chairs here in this town." My ridiculous thoughts were interrupted by a call from my husband. He was on his way to the game from work. "Where are you sitting?" he asked.

I laughed out loud and told him he wouldn't have any trouble spotting us. "You'll see. We are the family closest to the field."

Scott arrived in a little while, plopping down in the chair beside me. I gave him this big, old, goofy smile and asked, "Do we look dorky?"

"Pretty much," he said truthfully.

And there we sat, the three of us, for an entire soccer game. Too proud to move our chairs and too embarrassed to ask if we were in the wrong place. Just to make the situation more poignant, after the game was over, I walked to the row behind us and said hello to as many parents as I could. They looked at me like I had been invisible the entire game. Like they had never even seen me before. It is the weirdest feeling to realize, *Oh, I am invisible to you.*

Later, I began to ask myself, What did I want from the people sitting ten feet behind me? Why did that afternoon make me feel dumb? I knew that I didn't want any tangible thing from the other families. I didn't want a new best friend or to be invited over for dinner. I didn't want their money or a job. I didn't want their phone numbers or to go on vacation together.

Well then, what did you want? my head screamed. *I wanted to be noticed, included,* my honest heart replied. I just wanted someone to say, "Hey, come sit with us," or even, "Can I put my chair beside yours?" That's all. Just to belong to the soccer mom club, that's all my heart had wanted.

It's one thing to sit at a soccer game feeling unnoticed and disconnected. It's an even bigger deal to live most days not believing you are special enough to be known. Sometimes that's how this world makes us feel.

Becoming Invisible

I think that as a child, I always felt invisible. Along for the ride. Always taken care of but basically unseen. That's how most parents during our era believed children should be raised. Honestly, I never really gave it very much thought. Most of my friends grew up the same way. Cared for, but fairly invisible. My friends and I were all the same, hiding out in our forts after school, holed up in our bedrooms in the evening, running into the kitchen for supper, but otherwise alone and growing up in our private little worlds.

> *As a child, I always felt invisible—taken care of, but basically unseen.*

Completely opposite of my upbringing are two friends of mine who became child actors around ten years old. They tell me they have always been noticed and told they were special, but the pressure to become even more amazing was intense. And the microscopic focus on their lives was too much stress for a little kid. I think they might say they were seen but unknown. Their talent and beauty were applauded, but their hearts were left disconnected.

My college roommate and I used to joke, "Nobody knows we're here," because we would show up for gatherings only to stand at the edge of the room alone. Unspoken to. Back then it felt funny to say to each other, "We're invisible." But funny eventually wore off. Invisible is a lonely place for any woman on this earth.

Maybe the experience that taught me most about feeling invisible is being a mom. I had four babies, whom I am wildly in love with, in seven years. Ten years of changing diapers every single day. Lots of baby love. Lots of baby talk. Plenty of goo-goo, gaa-gaa. They became my world, and I didn't want it any other way. But what happens in those years is emotionally draining for anyone. Invisibility creeps in to cover your life. No one can see all that you do and the dreams that you dream. Except for God. He sees.

He sees you wander through the night retucking the princess sheets and superhero blankets. He stands with you in your laundry room, cheering for you as you match the endless socks and take the extra minutes to work on the newest stains. He knows that you struggle with the monotony of one day after another, each one exhausting and without a measurable accomplishment. Not only does God see, but maybe it would help you to know that He is filled with great pride over your sacrifice and your love. He watches how you care for the ones He has entrusted to you. When you give to those who will forget to say thank you, all of heaven stands to applaud you.

Being a single mom added yet another layer to my unseen life. The life of a mom is laden with hidden sacrifice and you wonder, Do they have any idea how much I care for them? Do they know who matched their socks and mopped the floor before they came to breakfast? Does anyone think that I'm special? Does my heart matter to anybody, really?

My children are a little older now, and the weariness changes, but the invisible work will probably never end. Before I sat down to write this morning, I took at least ten little things up to my youngest daughter's room because I knew she'd be sad if the puppies ate them. I paid the bills, took the untrained pups (the ones the kids begged us to have) outside at least four times, scheduled the orthodontist appointments, folded two loads of clothes, cleaned up from breakfast, loaded the dishwasher, scoured the refrigerator shelves where some orange juice had spilled, started the grocery list, sprayed for ants, texted my college girlfriends with some rah-rah words of encouragement, met with the yard man about removing a yard full of overgrown bushes, and grabbed the kids' piggy banks and deposit slips so they can add to their savings accounts at the bank after school. Invisible and unseen, at least on this earth. But so very noticed by God.

Truth is, you don't have to be a mom to feel invisible. I meet women all the time who struggle with different versions of this same ache. Friends of mine work faithfully at their desks, year after year, executing details, supporting corporate executives, wondering if anyone sees the value of their work beyond the paycheck they receive.

As I write to you today, I remember the women I've met who have known devastating physical abuse, rape, or incest. If you have lived through something similar, my dear friend, first let me tell you that I am so very, very sorry for every pain you have known. And I am incredibly angry that such horrific sin has been committed against you. Women tell me that such a tragedy can make you feel invisible, taking away the light in your life and your hope for the future.

Can I tell you what I know about God? He saw it all and He sees you now. He promises to be your Deliverer and your Healer. You are not invisible to Him, nor have you been assigned to live an invisible, broken life. God offers for-

> *Can I tell you what I know about God: He saw all the pain you suffered, and He sees you now. You are not invisible to Him.*

giveness to your offender, but for those who refuse to repent and trust in His Son, He promises a judgment.

I pray that you will know God's powerful presence today, that you will feel the love of God make you clean and new and that the light of Christ will fill your heart with His promise to give you a hope and a future (see Jeremiah 29:11).

Every weekend, I travel with some of the most unsung heroines of ministry. Women who spend long, long hours orchestrating women's conferences even years in advance. They travel to visit the venues, organize the endless details of hosting thousands of women for a weekend, stay up nights reworking what has fallen apart, and then graciously step into the shadows the day of the event, allowing God to take center stage and show up with His glory. Unseen. I wonder if they ask God, "Do You see what I have given?"

> "Am I a God who is near," declares the Lord, "And not a God
>   far off?"
> "Can a man hide himself in hiding places so I do not see him?"
>   declares the Lord.
> "Do I not fill the heavens and the earth?" declares the Lord.
>
> —Jeremiah 23:23–24 (NASB)

Women can live invisibly in their marriages, as neighbors—can be invisible even to their parents or their children. Relationships can make us ache with questions.

- Do you know who I am?
- Does anyone see the real me inside? Or the real pain I hide?
- Do you think I'm special?
- Am I worth the time it would take for you to see me?
- Would anyone want to pull up a chair and say, "Tell me who you are. What do you like? What makes you laugh? What dream do you dream?"

Because this world makes us feel so unnoticed, we sometimes begin to believe God can't see us either. Or maybe He just doesn't care. Or He has too much to do to pour Himself into the heart of one woman in her tiny corner of the world. So maybe your heart cries out, "Oh God, do You know that I am invisible? I am unseen. I am unknown." And then maybe your heart asks of the Lord, "Can You see me?"

I AM Your God Who Sees

The Old Testament gives us a story about a downcast woman named Hagar. We pick up her story in Genesis 16 with the narrative of Abram and Sarai. Before we learn more about Hagar, maybe it would help to have a little backstory.

God made a promise to Abram. He told Abram that he would have a son and that his descendents would outnumber the stars in the heavens. The Bible says that Abram believed God. But the years went by and no son ever came. So Abram's wife, Sarai, decided to take matters into her own hands and offered her maidservant, an Egyptian woman named Hagar, to him. You should know that in those days, Sarai's act wasn't considered immoral. By ancient custom, it was lawful for a barren wife to give a slave to her husband. But this act wasn't what God had ordained. Sarai was obviously trying to get ahead of the Lord. Sarai was like so many of us; she had misinterpreted God's delay as a denial and took matters into her own hands.

Hagar conceived with Abram, only to find Sarai horribly jealous during her pregnancy. The Scripture says, "Then Sarai mistreated Hagar; so she fled from her" (Genesis 16:6). Hagar's name means *flight*, and in the face of abuse and humiliation, she did exactly as her name implied. Hagar ran away, out into the desert of Egypt.

Hagar was in despair, hopeless, weary, alone, a woman in a male-dominated culture, pregnant, rejected, cast out after being used, surely feeling, *No one cares for me. No one understands.* Genesis 16:7 says, "The angel of the Lord found Hagar near a spring in the desert; it was the spring that is beside the road to Shur." I'm not sure where the road to Shur would have taken Hagar, but I am absolutely sure that she believed anywhere was better than the awful circumstances she was enduring. I am also sure that as she sat beside a spring in the middle of a desert, Hagar was incredibly alone. Unseen. Invisible to the people who knew her and surely believing she was invisible to God.

I don't know if your circumstances have ever made you want to run into a desert, but mine have. I've even made plans and told the kids many times, "We might just put it all up for sale, order homeschool books, and buy some clothes when we get to Africa. We're outta here." Course, they just stare at me like, "Silly ol' mom, she's so funny sometimes." But truly, there are days and seasons of life that make us want to run.

Maybe you have endured a judgment that made you want to evaporate. Just ask any Christian woman who has suffered through a divorce. She'll tell you what judgment feels like. Or ask the Christian woman who admits to having had an abortion, an affair, or an addiction. She knows that the heat of the desert seems mild compared to the heat of scandal, disgrace, and gossip.

> *The Christian woman who admits to having had an abortion, an affair, or an addiction knows that the heat of the desert seems mild compared to the heat of scandal, disgrace, and gossip.*

Maybe you haven't ever packed one bag, but you have run away in your heart. Disconnected from your husband. Your children. Your church. Maybe you have decided to endure those who have hurt you, but for all intents and purposes, you have run away. You and your hardened heart have put up a tent in the desert that is your life. Maybe you find yourself much like Hagar—alone, unsure, and wondering if anyone knows you're out there, and even if they knew, would they care?

Hagar must have been a miserable woman. Alone. Abused and mistreated. She must have asked God, "Do You see me down here? I have only done what was asked of me. I am pregnant and weary. No one will stand up for me, and this jealous woman is hurtful to me. None of this makes any sense. These are Your people, and I don't understand why they've treated me this way." She must have felt so very lost and confused.

I love that God stepped into her desert with His glory. Right to Hagar's side, God sent the "angel of the Lord," who many theologians believe to have been the very presence of His Son, Jesus. God saw Hagar. And God sees you and me. We are not invisible to Him.

When God Directs

The angel of the Lord came to Hagar with an instruction and a promise. *Instruction*: Go back to your mistress and submit to her (Genesis 16:9). *Promise*: I will so increase your descendants that they will be too numerous to count (verse 10).

The angel of God also gave Hagar a deep comfort by telling her that He saw her plight: "You are now with child and you will have a son. You shall name him Ishmael, for the Lord has heard of your misery" (verse 11).

Even though Hagar must have surely felt invisible to everyone, she encountered God in the most barren of places. God saw her loneliness and He heard her cries. God is a personal God, concerned about abused people and unborn babies. He cares for those who will trust Him. On this day in the desert, God not only saw her present pain; He also saw her future blessing because of her obedience.

I believe that God sees our heartache and our pain, and He desires to intervene in our lives with mercy, instruction, and promise. I also believe that many times in our own private deserts, the tears we cry when we cannot speak reach the heart of our Father as well as the prayers we are able to form with our minds.

> *Hagar gave this name to the Lord who spoke to her: "You are the God who sees me."*

After the angel of the Lord had compassionately spoken to Hagar, the Bible says, "She gave this name to the Lord who spoke to her: 'You are the God who sees me,' for she said, 'I have now seen the One who sees me'" (verse 13).

Hagar expressed her gratitude to God by naming Him El Roi, the God Who Sees. This occurrence began the Old Testament custom of giving a new name to God when He appeared to His people. The Bible goes on to say that Hagar marked the spot where she met God with a well called The One Who Lives and Sees. But probably Hagar's most important response was her obedience. She went back to Abram and Sarai, gave birth to Abram's son, Ishmael (whose name means "God hears"), and then lived in the promise of God's faithfulness.

Hagar was a downcast woman who encountered God in a life-changing way. I just can't help but believe God wants each one of us to know Him as "The God Who Sees." And even more wonderful, I believe the beautiful character of God has for us a fresh mercy, instruction, and a promise for our future.

God Sees You Too

Although she escaped from Abram and Sarai, Hagar did not escape "El Roi," the God Who Sees. In her darkest hour, God saw her need and heard her affliction. He knew right where she was, and He knew what she had been through. He came to Hagar, comforted her, gave her direction for survival, and spoke to her His promise of blessing.

My sister, whatever pain you carry or problem you endure, please know that El Roi, the God who sees, is there for you. He sees every tear; He hears every cry. He longs to heal your hurts.

This past weekend, a woman stood up to tell her story. I've actually heard a different version of this story almost every place I've gone. This woman told of her dark battle with depression. She described a heaviness akin to walking around with a "pillow strapped to my head" and a darkness that feels like light will never break through. As I listened to the details of her counseling, stays in the hospital, and necessary medication, I realized that in the dark parts of her soul, it must *feel* like God cannot see her brokenness. And if He does see, He must surely be frustrated with her ongoing depression and pain.

I don't know if you battle a similar depression or a darkness that comes and goes, but I want you to know our Father is truly *El Roi*. He sees the heavy heart you carry. He knows the past and all the wounds you have suffered. Even more, He sees the future and remembers His promise to save you.

> The LORD is close to the brokenhearted
> and saves those who are crushed in spirit.
>
> —PSALM 34:18

Maybe you have known an abuse—sexual, mental, or physical—that has already driven you into a lonely desert. I want you to know that there can be healing with God. Healing begins by recognizing that our God is *El Roi,* the God who sees. The Bible makes a promise to everyone who turns toward God. Psalm 9:10 says, "For you, LORD, have never forsaken those who seek you." God never forsakes any who call out to Him. He sees your pain and does not turn away.

Maybe you are living alone wondering if there is anyone in this world who sees the truth of your deep needs or the ache of locking yourself, alone, inside your home every night. I want you to know, God sees. And He has the power to give you a comfort and a peace that no one else could ever give to you. God also sees how you long to be loved. How you'd just like a hand to hold. How much you want to share the good and the hard with someone who cares. My sister, I have been you. But we must hang on to the truth that He hears your prayers, stands guard around your home, protects your future, and directs your path. He rescues, redeems, and heals. Just hold on, my friend.

As I am writing to you this morning, I sense God's sweet pleasure over all that we give with integrity and grace. It's like He whispers to us, "Hey, baby, I see you! Through the good and the bad, the accomplishment and the disappointment, I am with you always. Never far away. I am your biggest fan and wildly shout *Bravo* every time you give and try and succeed. I am also your source of strength and your place of healing. I am your shelter and your soft place to fall. Your weakness does not push Me away. I am here. I see what you need. I promise to keep all My promises to you."

I am your shelter and your soft place to fall.

Maybe today you need to know God is near. That all of heaven is coming to your rescue. That the Source of every hope sees your circumstances and your pain. Take a moment wherever you are to incline your heart to God. Ask Him, "Do You see me?" Now wait to hear His answer.

Knowing God Sees

Many years ago, when I was living as a single mom, God sent a beautiful gift into my life. Her name was Beverly. My friend Carla thought I needed help keeping my house in order (and I did), so she sent Beverly—the woman who helped her family—over to help me. At first Beverly came every couple of weeks, and eventually she said to me, "I know you need help every week, so what if I only charge you fifty dollars a week, then I'll come and do everything I can get done in four hours." I had no idea what a blessing Beverly would become to me, nor did I have any idea what kind of spiritual lessons God had in store for my whole family.

Beverly did just fine at cleaning. In the eight years she came to our house, I can't ever remember her missing a week. She would rush right in the back door and begin working her plan. She'd strip the beds and get the wash going, then attack the rest of the house in a matter of hours. Not only did I get to know Beverly through the years because I worked at home, she came to know all of us, and the children talked about her like she was an angel who hovered over our family.

The more I think about it, the more I think Beverly could have been an angel. One of the spiritual lessons I learned from Beverly is that she believed in El Roi, the God Who Sees. She was always mindful that God sees everything and is personally involved in our lives. Every day she came to my house, I listened as she responded to Him with the most intimate knowledge of His presence I've ever encountered. I don't know if Beverly had much formal education, but she was very smart about God. God was always present to her, speaking to her and guiding her about how to pray for us.

You see, I thought Beverly came every week simply to clean our house, but now I believe God sent her to clean in the spirit. Beverly would sing hymns, loudly, all over the house as she worked. She prayed out loud as she moved through the rooms. Every week she lay on my children's beds facedown and prayed for that child before she replaced the fresh sheets. I'd hear her talking to God and laughing at His response to her. One day I heard a commotion at the front door, and I walked around the corner to see what was going on. Beverly told me she was spitting on the devil.

"He thinks he can just come in this house, and I told him, 'In the name of Jesus,' to leave you alone." Then she showed me how she had yelled, "Phooey on the devil," and pretended to spit all around the room to make her point. I had to keep myself from laughing out loud watching her "spit on the devil" in my foyer; but the more I thought about it, the more I agreed with her. People ought to spit on the devil.

Another day, she came into my office and asked how I was doing. I have no idea what I told her, but my heart was heavy as I explained something that was going on. Beverly came over to me and said, "Angela, get down on your knees." So I did. The next thing I knew, she was bent over me praying Scripture, spitting on the devil, calling on all of heaven to come and minister to God's servant. Then, as I stayed kneeling, she danced around the room, singing, praying, and laughing. All this, mind you, with a feather duster in her right hand just like it was a scepter from heaven. When she was finished and she felt God had answered, she told me to get up. And I did. I may be the Bible teacher, but when Beverly, the housekeeper who loves God, told me to get down on my knees, I listened.

Beverly's style of worship and prayer is so different from mine. I have been an uptight worshipper most of my life, and even though Beverly and I were outwardly very different, I came to respect her love and deep commitment to God. Beverly lived in one of the wildest displays of faith I've ever encountered. I'm sure you could have guessed she had fiery red hair that she was incredibly proud of. She loved that her blazing spiritual life matched her brilliant, beautiful hair. She was truly one of the most passionate women I have ever, to this day, encountered. I had the great, great privilege of being in the same house with her every Wednesday for about eight years. Even today, I can almost hear her telling me something like this: "Girl, I woke up this morning, and the Lord was sitting at the foot of my bed. He'd just been smiling over me while I slept, waiting to pour out the blessing of a new day. He whispered to me how beautiful I am to Him. He told me He would protect me today, and then He gave me the plan for the morning. I just laughed over how good He is to me. I praised Him for loving me so much. I told Him how much I need Him. We started the day together, me and God. He rode here with me this morning. I am never unseen by God."

It didn't take me long to realize that I wanted a passionate faith like Beverly's. I wanted to be a woman who knows she is not invisible to God. Thanks, in part, to Beverly, I am growing in the freedom and beauty of worship. I think the Lord had much to teach this reserved academic about my "God Who Sees."

Living in His Sight

After she had encountered the God Who Sees, I imagine that Hagar returned to her mistress, Sarai, a different woman. She probably went back to their village looking a little more like Beverly and a little less like the downcast woman she had been.

You hear me saying, "God is here. He sees your life. You are not invisible to Him!" But how can we live in the power of this truth about the God Who Sees? What would it take for us to live in the reality that God is present? Alive. Powerful. Right beside us. What needs to happen in our hearts to respond so organically to God's leading?

Here are a few of the things Beverly taught me about living in His sight.

Live Grateful
See God in every gift, big and small, that comes to you. Thank God first. Remember that every good and perfect gift comes from our God who sees.[1]

Live Tenderly
Respond to God when He prompts you. Since I want God to speak to me, and because I know that God sees me, I need to be faithful to quickly obey. Acts 8:26–27 says, "Now an angel of the Lord said to Philip, 'Go south to the road—the desert road—that goes down from Jerusalem to Gaza.' So he started out. . . ."

A heart that is tender toward God helps us respond to His instruction like Philip did. God directs, and we immediately start out to do what He has said.

Live in Prayer
Ask the Lord, instead of your to-do list, to direct your day. Listen for the still, small voice of God. Respond in obedience. Today might be an accomplishment day or it might be a give-yourself-away kind of day. In prayer, we hear God tell us which way to go.

Live with Eyes Wide Open
Hagar said she had seen the God who sees. My friend Beverly lived with her spiritual eyes wide open to see God too. May we see our great, big God so very present and real. I pray the eyes of your heart may be enlightened in order that you may know.[2]

No matter where today finds you: Feeling invisible at the soccer game. Invisible in your own home. Or invisible in the depths of a dark depression. Call on El Roi. He is our God Who Sees.

❀

Does your heart cry out,
"God, do You know I am invisible?"
Then listen as our Lord as He replies to your invisible heart:

Do you know who I am? . . .
I AM the God who sees.

My eyes move all across the earth so that I can strengthen those whose
hearts are fully committed to Me. I look to the ends of the earth and
see everything under the heavens. My eyes are on your ways, and
I see all your steps. I look from heaven and see all who inhabit the
earth. My daughter, don't forget that I AM the One who fashioned
your heart. I AM the One who understands all your works.

There is nowhere you can run from My presence. I AM wherever
you are. Darkness cannot overwhelm you because darkness is not
dark to me. For me, the night is as bright as the day. My eyes are on
the righteous. I see what you give and pray and fast in secret. You are
not invisible to me. I AM your Guardian God. I will not let your foot
slip, neither will I fall asleep or slumber. I will be your guard when
you leave and when you return. I am the guardian who watches over
you now and always.

> *You are my beloved and I AM your God who sees*
> *Forever and ever, amen.*[3]

When anxiety was great within me,
your consolation brought joy to my soul.
—PSALM 94:19

CHAPTER THREE

DO YOU KNOW
I AM TREMBLING INSIDE?

He Is My Comfort

This could be cervical cancer.

"We'll need to schedule a more involved procedure to investigate further," my doctor said to me a couple of weeks ago.

Oh.

Hmmm.

I think I smiled at the doctor even as I sat there fairly stunned. *I guess he's talking to me*, my numb self realized.

The "more involved" test is scheduled for a week from Monday. But here I am this afternoon, standing at the edge of bad news. Actually, it's the edge of bad news with options. In one direction is a cliff where I could jump off into awful news. And in the other direction is a pasture where I could run and turn cartwheels of relief. We won't know which way this news goes until I have the procedure and then results from the pathology lab. So, until then, I'm at the edge. I am waiting between the now and *Whew, it was nothing*. Or possibly, I'm waiting between the now and *Oh no, here we go*.

Maybe you've heard something that left you frozen and dazed. A test result that indicates cancer. The 401(k) statement that your husband deciphered aloud. A layoff notice read grimly to your entire department. Or the text from a child to tell you they didn't mean to, they're sorry, but they've been arrested. News that takes your breath away and instantly numbs your soul with dread.

Maybe you are standing at the edge of bad news, wondering, *How did something so big just sneak into my life and speak to me through a calm voice?* Maybe you are asking God, "Do You know how I feel right now? Do You know that I am totally shocked by this? And I'm trembling inside? And confused about why? Oh Lord, Your baby girl just went weak with fear. Do You know that I am afraid?"

I could wait to write this chapter until the pathology results are in. Then if they're all clear, I could try to remember how it feels today at the edge of bad news and write to you after I've turned cartwheels. But I decided that it matters more to write now, at the edge, and in the waiting. I want the lessons of these days. I want to know God right now, in this. More than anything on this earth, I want to live what I believe. So today, as you read my words to you, no matter what fear has come to you, I want you to know I am with you. Fear is sitting across the desk from me, begging me to give him my attention. I hear his taunts. I know he is present. But I am determined to know my God more.

> *I hear Fear's taunts. I know he is present. But I am determined to know my God more.*

I drove away from the doctor's office with appointment reminders on my lap, thinking, *I did not see this coming.* No symptoms. Not one pain or ache. Nothing to warn me that my doctor could have bad news. In the few miles to my house, my humanity kicked in and anxiousness began to build. I vividly remember the trembling inside, a jittery, hand-shaking kind of trembling as I fumbled through the motions of driving myself home.

And then the wild thoughts whispered by Fear began to swirl through my head. You know the thoughts I'm talking about, the regular, run-of-the-mill wild thoughts about leaving my children motherless, missing out on the amazing marriage I planned to have with my hunky man, and the other stuff that goes along with losing your mind while you stand at the edge of bad news. I was just a normal, ordinary woman, responding like every other woman on this earth. *I don't want to have cancer.* And then the firstborn chimed in, *And I don't have* time *to have cancer either.*

I have walked with God for a very long time, and obviously, this is not the first time I have heard bad news. I will never forget being in the Pittsburgh airport when my daddy called to say the tests just came back and Mama had ovarian cancer, stage 3-C. I remember that same numb, sick feeling that came over me and the tears that instantly spilled from my eyes. Overcome with a deep ache for Mama, I wept openly in the gate area where I was waiting. I will also never forget the complete stranger, a lady who came over and put her arms around me and held me until I could speak.

I think every single time bad news bursts in on an otherwise really great day, our soul reacts with spontaneous grief and deeply vulnerable pain. It's the way we were created. We are supposed to feel, and to ache over sadness is human.

On my drive home from the doctor's office that day, no one miraculously appeared in the passenger seat next to me to hold me. I couldn't get my husband on the phone, so I drove along quietly. But the sweetest thing happened anyway. God came. Really. I kind of wanted to cry over my doctor's bad news. My eyes were stinging. But no tears came. I was getting ready to pray, but I hadn't even begun praying in earnest, yet still I knew God was present. In my car. He was powerfully present. How did I know? The deepest peace took hold of my trembling insides and everything inside of me—heart, soul, and physical body—was at ease. Completely still. The trembling just stopped.

I had assumed I would go home and work through all the details of my doctor's visit, pray them out, study the Scriptures, and talk to some godly friends; then I'd wait until that path of seeking God led me to a peace about the tests for cancer. But instead, God just breathed a peace over me in an instant. He gave in a moment more than I even knew to ask for. It was, and is, exactly the kind of peace that Paul wrote about to the Philippians: "And the peace of God, which transcends all understanding, will guard your hearts and your minds in Christ Jesus" (4:7).

I love how Eugene Peterson paraphrases this powerful truth:

> Before you know it, a sense of God's wholeness, everything
> coming together for good, will come and settle you down. It's
> wonderful what happens when Christ displaces worry at the
> center of your life.
>
> —PHILIPPIANS 4:7 (MESSAGE)

That morning, only a few days ago, God graciously met me in my car and came to settle down all that was trembling inside.

I said to the Lord, "Do You know who I am right now? Do You know that I'm trembling inside?" and He came with the power of who He is. It was as if He whispered, "Do you remember who you belong to? Do you know that I am your comfort?"

Living Alongside Trouble

I believe that cancer and catastrophes and awful consequences show their presence in our lives because we live in a fallen world. No one gets a free pass. There are no immunity idols to help us become survivors on this journey. There is only one way with God, and that is to believe that we cannot save ourselves. Our only way is to believe that God's Son, Jesus, truly lived, died, and rose again to save us from this world.

Saved. It's an old-fashioned word straight out of the Bible, but nothing gives me more comfort than its everlasting truth.

I am saved.

Saved from eternal death and suffering.

Saved for heaven, forever.

Saved from more bondage to my sin on this earth.

Saved because God is love and not because I did anything to deserve it.

In the book of Acts, the honest question is asked, "What must I do to be saved?" And the very simple, beautiful answer is written, "Believe in the Lord Jesus, and you will be saved" (Acts 16:30–31).

Today you can tell Jesus that you believe He is the Savior, that you believe He paid for your sin with His death, and that you believe He is the only way to eternal life. My friend, if I could give you anything, I'd give you the grace to believe in Jesus. His love toward me is my only hope and my only peace. Believing is the only path to real comfort. So today, would you believe that Jesus loves you too and that He died to be your Savior?

I'd love to tell you more with some videos at www.angelathomas.com/saved.

This very weekend I sat with a woman before the start of a conference. She told me that her husband is a stockbroker and she works in his office. Through her tears she said, "We've lost everything. I'm not sure if we'll even have a business in two months." Then she continued, "I don't understand. My husband has done everything right. He has run his business with integrity. He has tithed and financially taken care of my family and his. I thought when you lived right, things turned out right."

I held her hands and told her I was so very sorry for their loss. I went on to tell her that not one of Jesus' disciples escaped this lifetime without suffering. They didn't model for us an insulated life, free of heartache and pain. Jesus reminded His disciples and us in John 16:33, "In this world you will have trouble."

Not one of Jesus' disciples escaped this lifetime without suffering.

The Son of God Himself suffered an unimaginable death, even though He lived a flawless life. And so, who am I to think that somehow I just might skip past adversity? It will not happen. It won't happen for any of us.

So today, many of us who are faithful followers of Christ stand at the edge of bad news, learning how to ask God for a comfort that we never wanted to need.

Here's an update on my journey with my cancer procedures: I had the "more involved" procedure yesterday in my doctor's office. Obviously we were all praying that he would find nothing and that we'd step away from this edge of bad news. Unfortunately, my gynecologist saw two areas that he believes to be precancerous. He has taken biopsies and now the report from those tests is about eight days away. The results could say mild, moderate, or severely precancerous. The result could also be positive for cervical cancer. And so I wait. And while I wait, I pursue this beautiful, promised comfort of God.

We, the redeemed of God, have been assigned to live on this earth, in these days, right beside what is evil and tainted. But we were made for so much more. Our hearts long for the perfect presence of God and the perfect bodies that will worship Him completely. But until then, the questions remain: Oh God, do You know that I am trembling at the mention of this disease? And do You know that I feel afraid of all the possible implications? I was going to be so brave, if my day of sorrow ever came. But this afternoon I am sure that You are the only One who can see the depth of my weakness, and You are the only One who can be brave enough for me.

I AM Your God Who Gives Comfort

Over and over again, God keeps taking me to a passage written by Paul to the Christ followers in Corinth, 2 Corinthians 1:3–11. To be honest with you, I wanted to turn to a different place in the Bible, and I truly kept trying to study something else. Maybe a chapter in the Psalms where the writer asks God to remove his affliction. Maybe a miraculous healing passage. Or a selection on overcoming fear where angels appear with glory to bring calm to the petrified. But God has led me here, to a very honest chunk of verses. And a great, big truth about our God. This passage is a little like what my mama would call a "horse pill." Something so big you are sure you will never be able to swallow it, but so powerfully healing for your body that you know it's the best thing for you.

In this letter, the writer, Paul, doesn't focus on himself or his adversity. He says God uses our suffering and His divine comfort to turn us outward toward a hurting world. Not one word about removing the suffering before it gets too bad or hurts too much, which is kind of what I was hoping to read. But very powerful words about God's character and His promise for us.

Let's jump in together and see what God does when we are trembling inside. Paul begins this passage with praise and a vivid reminder about who God is: "Blessed be the God and Father of our Lord Jesus Christ, the Father of mercies and God of all comfort" (2 Corinthians 1:3, NASB).

Do we remember who our God is? He is the Father of all mercy and the God of all comfort. I hear Him reminding me right now, "Do you know I AM your mercy for every medical report and every phone call you receive? Do you know I AM your comfort for every minute and every surprise this day holds?"

Not one word about removing the suffering before it gets too bad or hurts too much.

I love how the great classic writer Hannah Whitall Smith defined comfort:

Comfort, whether human or divine, is pure and simple comfort, and is nothing else. We none of us care for pious phrases, we want realities; and the reality of being comforted and comfortable seems to me almost more delightful than any other thing in life. We all know what it is. When as little children we have cuddled up into our mother's lap after a fall or a misfortune, and have felt her dear arms around us, and her soft kisses on our hair, we have had comfort. When, as grown-up people, after a hard day's work, we have put on our slippers and seated ourselves by the fire, in an easy chair with a book, we have had comfort. When, after a painful illness, we have begun to recover, and have been able to stretch our limbs and open our eyes without pain, we have had comfort. . . . In that word comfortable there has been comprised more of rest, and relief, and satisfaction, and pleasure, than any other word in the English language could possibly be made to express. We cannot fail, therefore, to understand the meaning of this name of God, the "God of all comfort."[1]

Our God is the source of comfort, which means that He is the factory where mercy and comfort are manufactured. Anytime you encounter a mercy or a comfort, it found its beginning in the character of our heavenly Father. Maybe we can think about God's comfort like this:

> We must not think of *comfort* in terms of "sympathy," because sympathy can weaken us instead of strengthen us. God does not pat us on the head and give us a piece of candy or a toy to distract our attention from our troubles. No, He puts strength into our hearts so we can face our trials and triumph over them.[2]

It is interesting to me that in the past few weeks, people have said many gracious things because they wanted to give me comfort and encouragement. Several times I have heard, "I'm just gonna pray this is nothing," which is very sweet, except that three medical tests are saying this is something real. So what was intended as comfort seems to encourage denial. And honestly, living in the fake land of denial would make me even more afraid.

But most of my friends and family have said to me, "First, we're gonna pray for the least possible bad result and next, we're gonna fight for you like crazy people, no matter what happens." I loved hearing something like that. It is humbling to have people stand with you and say they'll fight for you. My tender-hearted husband tells me every day, "I am going to take care of you." The support and prayers of people I love is a very real strength to me. I am so grateful to be covered by their compassion.

What was intended as comfort seems to encourage denial.

But these past weeks, the deep soul comfort, the kind of comfort that makes your inside be still and clears your mind of ridiculous exaggerations, has come to me in the presence of God. Alone in my car when my spirit is searching for His; lying on my bedroom floor and praying over Scriptures. Worshipping last Sunday and singing at the top of my voice, "Hail to the King, power and strength are yours alone, Hail to the King." In the presence of God, I have been able to take a deep breath and hear myself say from a genuine place of assurance, "No matter what comes, I do know I belong to God. Cancer or not, I will be okay in His arms."

Maybe your heart needs comfort too. Or maybe there is someone you love who needs more than your compassion can give . . . he or she needs a deep, abiding comfort that gives a real peace. Here are some thoughts about seeking the I AM comfort of God:

- Separate yourself from everyone else's input so that you can be alone with God. You may actually be receiving brilliant advice from people you respect, but that deep, abiding comfort that your soul longs for will come only from God. A soul quiet with Him. Room to hear. A place to be still and know.
- Let yourself cry freely if the tears want to come. Sometimes I think we have to cry it out so that we can hear. After I have cried out my pain, it seems like I can hear God speaking so much more clearly.
- Meditate on some of these passages. Journal if you want. Let these verses become your own prayers, substituting your name where you can.

Psalm 27:4–6	Psalm 121
Isaiah 40:28–31	John 14:27
Romans 8:26	Romans 8:38–39
1 Peter 1:3–9	1 Peter 5:6–7
- Ask people to pray that you would receive God's comfort.

It turns out that our God knows how we tremble over bad news. He alone is the One who can soothe our troubled hearts. Does your heart need God's mercy today? Are you searching for a comfort that you cannot produce for yourself? Maybe the well-meaning words of your friends have fallen flat on your anxiousness. According to Paul's words, we have a Father who promises deep and enduring comfort for every pain. He gives a strength that miraculously soothes our trembling knees and troubled thinking.

The Purpose of Receiving Comfort

God gives comfort to the deepest parts of our souls, and with that comfort, He has an even bigger purpose. Let's look at God's plan: "[He] comforts us in all our troubles, *so that* we can comfort those in any trouble with the comfort we ourselves have received from God" (2 Corinthians 1:4, italics added).

Amazing. As much as pain makes us want to retreat and hide, Paul says we're supposed to receive the mercy of God's comfort and then turn toward a hurting world with all that has been given to us. Good grief. A selflessness right in the middle of great suffering. It's just like God to say, "Use your suffering to help someone else. Take the truth of My character to those who are hurting." And then He gives us the grace to make it happen. The idea is that the more comfort we have received from God, the more we will be able to comfort others. Comfort multiplied through the honesty of the hurting.

The more comfort we have received from God, the more we will be able to comfort others.

Paul prayed that his comfort would give others who suffer a "patient endurance" (2 Corinthians 1:6). Patient endurance is an evidence of faith. It's also the mark of spiritual maturity.

Maybe the comfort I can give today would sound something like this:

I heard you just received some bad news. Me too. I know how that kind of thing makes you chase after your breath. It feels like the world stands still for a moment and your mind begins to race, trying to take all the words in. I want you to know what God has done for me. He hasn't taken away my news, at least not yet, but He has truly come to comfort me with the power of His enduring love.

He keeps reminding me that He is absolutely in charge of all the circumstances that concern me. He keeps telling me that He is my deliverer and my friend. I can't even understand how this is happening, but He is miraculously taking away my fears and my anxiousness. I feel myself putting the full weight of my need securely into His hands. I am leaning into God, and somehow—it's still a mystery to me—God is giving me grace to endure and believe Him. Can I pray that our God will come and do the same for you?

As you think about the purpose of comfort, ask God to show you who might need a comfort you can give today.

I love that as Paul is writing this letter to other believers, he doesn't see the need to cover his real feelings and fears. He is vulnerable and honest. He knows that in our weakness, others can see the strength of God. He says, "We were under great pressure, far beyond our ability to endure, so that we despaired even of life. Indeed, in our hearts we felt the sentence of death" (2 Corinthians 1:8).

As I reread these words from the apostle, I decided this must have been how my mom felt midway through her chemotherapy for ovarian cancer. About three awful treatments into the process, she began to say, "I cannot do this again." Her body was so very weak, and we all knew she meant it with every devastated fiber in her body. She didn't believe she could go on. But somehow, some way, days would pass between the chemo, and God would give her a fresh mercy so that she could return to the hospital to take the next IV drip of what she called "the poison." My mom was far beyond her ability to endure. We are all certain it was only the I AM comfort of God that brought her through.

Paul did not deny the way he felt; neither does God want us to deny our emotions. We just can't help how our humanity responds to heartache and suffering. The physical body gasps for air when we are in need, and the spiritual body gasps for grace when we are in need. We do not have to deny the honest fears, but we can choose to turn our humanity and our need toward our Savior.

Do you know a pressure far beyond your ability to endure? Does your circumstance make you despair, even of life? In your heart, have you felt the sentence of death? Then Paul is giving you and me the very same comfort that he received from God.

Now look at Paul's understanding of his despair: "But this happened that we might not rely on ourselves but on God" (2 Corinthians 1:9). Maybe you are a little like me. Just about the first thing I do when I encounter a trial is to rely on myself. I mean, I hop on the Internet to research solutions and procedures. I call people, go through a mental checklist of what seems like a logical approach. Truly, I immediately try to rely on myself. But when the trouble is so big, so big that we even despair for our lives, Paul says that our overwhelming need teaches us to rely on God. He is the only hope we have anyway.

Learning to Trust Him More

I have trusted God in the dark so many times in my life, standing beside a lake where my sister drowned, wading through huge financial pressures for many years, standing in the dark through my divorce, the seven years I lived as a single mom, the months my mom battled ovarian cancer. And yet this new lesson of trust means I am being stretched, always learning how to trust God more.

Here is the point with God: We cannot store up reserves of grace and warehouses of trust. As our suffering increases, so does God's supply. If we could store up grace for emergency use, we might be more inclined to trust in ourselves and our hoard of grace, rather than trusting in the fresh mercies of God. It's interesting that most of the earthly resources God gives to us can be stored for future use—money, food, knowledge, and so on—but His grace cannot be stored away. We are completely dependent on this day's encounter with the endless supply of God's grace. God's character toward me and you is full of the comfort. But His comfort is increased through faith. Learning to trust His character more means receiving a deeper comfort every time we lean into His strength a little more.

We cannot store up reserves of grace and trust. As our suffering increases, so does God's supply.

God wants us to *live* the truths of Scripture, not just recount our knowledge of them. In these days I am relearning how to *live* these truths about God:

- When more grace is needed . . . He gives more grace. (See James 4:6.)

- When I am weak . . . then I am strong because of Him. (See 2 Corinthians 12:10.)
- Suffering perfects my character. (See Romans 5:1–5.)
- I can be confident that God truly gives grace and mercy in a time of need. And if I need more tomorrow, He will be faithful to give. (See Hebrews 4:16.)

God wants me and you to trust *Him.* Just Him. The Lord, God Almighty. Sovereign. Omniscient. Loving. Faithful. We are not to trust in our gifts or abilities or experience—not even our spiritual knowledge. He wants us to trust only in Him. To believe in His character. To be certain that His commitment to us is pure and good and eternal. To fully set our hope in who He is.

Paul writes: "On him we have set our hope that he will continue to deliver us" (2 Corinthians 1:10). God does not always deliver us immediately, nor does He deliver each of us in the same way. A commentator has said, "Sometimes God delivers us *from* our trials, and at other times He delivers us *in* our trials."[3] God has a multitude of ways He could choose to deliver me: through medicine, surgery, a miracle healing, or even being delivered into a new body in heaven. My responsibility is to put my hope in His character and in His care for me. That truly gives me comfort and peace.

The most important thing about seeking the comfort of God is fixing your attention on Him and not on yourself. Paul says that he "set" his hope on God. He made a conscious decision to put his hope fully in the Lord. You and I have to make the same intentional choice. We must remember where to look.

Knowing God's Presence
When I Am Afraid

My son William is thirteen. He is one of the all-time best kids on the planet. We call him Renaissance because he loves so many things. He follows Jesus with a tender heart, is great with schoolwork, plays the tenor sax. He's a little soccer star. And the kid gets in the car every day after school, swipes my phone, and checks the stock market, telling me which shares he should have bought yesterday.

Almost every other sentence out of William is about an invention. This morning he wanted to install some kind of device on teenagers' cars so that they would not be allowed to drive more than ten miles above the speed limit, and this device would automatically know the speed limit wherever the student is, based on GPS tracking. That same satellite tracking would also alert the young driver to stop signs and traffic concerns ahead. Obviously, his mind is always whirling.

But my little Renaissance man has one fear. William, at this age, feels anxious when he is alone. He has grown up in a big family with lots of people, so he's never really had to be alone. And as brave and smart as he is about almost everything else, my sweet William says being alone just makes him feel afraid.

This morning I needed to be at the airport around eight. The kids are out of school and everyone else is away with a friend except William. Last night, I knew what the answer was going to be before I asked, but I said, "William, do you want to sleep in tomorrow morning since you don't have school, then Scott will come home after he takes me to the airport? Or do you want to get up and go with us?" Without hesitation, he wanted to get up early. My boy doesn't like to be alone.

As I've thought about William's fear, I have realized that my desire to parent and love him well is only a poor imitation of our heavenly Father's matchless love for us. Anything good that I feel for William as a parent has been perfected by God and given to us as our Father. I want to give William comfort and peace for his tender heart. Even more perfectly, our heavenly Father gives to us a deep and soothing comfort that no one else in this world can give. As I think about how I care about William's one little fear, it makes more aware of the father-character of our God and teaches me so much about how He responds to us when we are trembling inside.

Some of the things I have realized as a mom who wants to give comfort are:

I am not mad at my son for being afraid. He is a little boy, not yet a man, and I am his mom. Even more perfectly, God is not mad at us when we tremble inside. He knows the limitations of our humanity. He created us with earthly minds and emotions. He is not mad when we come to Him with our fears. The Bible says God has compassion on our weakness and longs for us to turn toward Him for our comfort.

When I sense that William is fearful, I go to him. He is a snuggle-bunny, and hugs make him feel safe. I'm a lot like that too. Very touchy-feely, hug-hug. It's my love language, and I think I've passed it to most of the family. Scripture says God is near to the broken-hearted. I believe that even more than an earthly parent would run to comfort his or her child, our Father runs to us, His children. He gives us a comfort we cannot receive apart from Him. He is present. He is our refuge. Our safety. Our hiding place.

Nothing William could do, no fear that he could have, would ever make me love him less. Romans 8 says nothing can ever separate us from the love of God, not our fears, not our trembling. Not even our confusion about the heartaches that come into our lives. Even when we push Him away with our cries, He does not withdraw His love or dangle it cruelly just out of reach. No honest feeling or thought will ever diminish the love of God for you.

The Significance of God's Character

God is comfort. This morning as I write, my soul sighs, *Hallelujah.* I am married to one of the most beautiful, compassionate men you will ever meet, but his sweet words to me cannot compare to knowing God as my comfort. It's the same with my parents, my children, and the friends who say all the right and loving things. I am grateful for them all, but my trembling finds its rest in my Father.

One thing I am sure of is that my God sees me and He sees you. He knows my fears before I can name them. He sees when I am standing at the edge of bad news, and He comes to draw me closer.

Today, I want you to know that God is your comfort. Whatever has come to trouble your spirit. Whatever physical challenge you face. The stress of your deadlines, the choices one of your children has made, or the uncertain financial future you face. Wherever your soul trembles, call on our God, who makes a promise to be true to His character—He gives comfort in all of our troubles.

Let me share a brief note from my journey: My doctor called last night with great, great news. My precancerous cells are still present, but the pathology result says they are in the mild stages. I will have a freezing procedure in the next couple of weeks to remove those layers of cells. Then my physician will monitor me closely the next six months. To be honest with you, I am thrilled, but the thinking part of me has been preparing for the worst news. I have been reading about radical hysterectomies and looking at my schedule to see when I could fit one in. I am so very grateful. This is what I had hoped for, but based on my family history with cancer, not what I was expecting. Hallelujah!

Remembering

I believe that the only way to experience the true comfort of God is to believe everything He has written to us in the Scriptures. And if you are anything like me, it's not that you don't believe, it's that many times, in our pain or in our hurried, stressful lives, we forget to remember.

I want to remember *who* God has been to me these last weeks. When a trouble comes to you, I want you to remember as well. He has reminded me that He is my deep well of mercy, my Father of Comfort (2 Corinthians 1:3).

> Divine comfort does not come to us in any mysterious or
> arbitrary way. It comes as the result of a divine method. The
> indwelling Comforter "brings to our remembrance" comforting
> things concerning our Lord, and, if we believe them, we are
> comforted by them.
>
> —Hannah Whitall Smith[4]

I want to remember what *He did* when I was trembling and afraid. God came to me. His presence in my car gave me a peace I could not describe. The truth of His promises in Scripture came flooding back to me, and I remembered that God is faithful. I said out loud over and over, "I trust God and believe that no matter the outcome, I am held and protected by God."

I want to remember what *God does through me*. He is so clear in His instruction. "Angela, go and give the comfort I have given to you. Tell anyone who is in need that I give peace beyond understanding. Tell them how I gave peace on the day you received bad news. Tell them I am waiting to comfort all who turn toward Me."

I will not forget the God who knows me. The God who comforts me. The same God who holds each breath in the palm of His hand.

Does your heart cry out,
"God, do You know I am trembling inside?"
Then listen as our Lord speaks to your trembling heart:

DO YOU KNOW WHO I AM?
I AM the God of all comfort.

As a mother comforts her child, so will I comfort you. My love is as tender and true as a mother's comfort, so I want you to believe in Me and rest in the genuine peace I can give to you. My peace is different than this world's peace. Do not let your heart be troubled and do not be afraid.

Remember who I AM and believe in my character. I AM the One who gives comfort to all. Have you forgotten who stretched out the heavens and laid the foundations of the earth?

I love you so much that I sent My Son, Jesus, to show you how to believe in who I AM. I have anointed Him to heal your broken heart, to release sinners from their bondage, and to comfort all who mourn. I have seen your sin, but I have sent Jesus to heal you of your ways, to make your heart clean and restore comfort to your soul. His love is big and deep and wide and high so that My comfort will reach even you.

I AM the God who comforts the downcast. And I AM not far off. I have also sent the Comforter, who is the Holy Spirit. He is with you always. Ever present. Never leaving. Never failing. This Comforter will teach you spiritual things and keep reminding you of who I AM.

My comfort will calm your anxiety and bring joy to your soul. Let the love of Jesus come to you and bring you an everlasting comfort. And from that comfort, let your heart be encouraged and your life strengthened for every good word and work that I have planned for you.

Rely on Me and then give others what I have given to you. Comfort someone else with the comfort you have received from Me. My plans for you are good. And in all these things I will receive the glory.

You are my beloved, and I AM your comfort. Forever and ever, amen.[5]

I will refresh the weary and satisfy the faint.
—JEREMIAH 31:25

CHAPTER FOUR

DO YOU KNOW
I AM WORN OUT?

He Does Not Grow Weary

I took a nap today.

Twenty minutes sounded like exactly what I needed for a little shut-eye. I hoped a nap would restore my soul, untangle my overwhelmed schedule, replenish my weary body, and, all in all, just make me a more delightful person. I always have such high hopes about a nap.

So I set the alarm on my phone and then, fully dressed, lay across the top of the bed. But my phone rang at twelve minutes in, just as I had fallen into the "I think I'm sleeping" phase. It was one of the children. I thought I should take it. My nap was over.

> I am worn to a raveling.
>
> —BEATRIX POTTER, *The Tailor of Gloucester*

Maybe I should have spent those twelve minutes outside pulling weeds. At least there would be fewer weeds. My micronap only left me yawning. No real benefit. No miraculous transformation. Just the same old me. Still so very tired. And totally in over my head.

I guess one comfort I have is that I believe your life is a lot like mine. Everybody I know is flat worn out. Pooped. The only people I know who are rested are my parents. They just spent four months in Florida, sleeping until ten, eating what they wanted, sitting in the sun, and taking naps. Maybe they aren't worn out now, but they have been. They lived like I do times twenty when we were growing up. Their rested faces give me hope that one day it will be our turn too. But today, yesterday, next week . . . it's not my turn. I may not get my turn until heaven.

> *My heart whispers to God, "Do*
> *You know that I am worn out?*
> *Do You see how hard I'm trying?*
> *Do You know I can't keep up?"*

My heart whispers to God, "Do You know that I am worn out? Do You see how hard I'm trying? Do you know I can't keep up? That there is more to be done than ten of me could accomplish? Oh Lord, do You know?"

> The man declares, "I am *weary*, O God; I am *weary*, O God, and worn out."
>
> —Proverbs 30:1 (ESV italics added)

This past weekend I read a book written for women who are worn out. I hoped it would have all the answers. The authors are Christians. I loved the title and concept. I imagine the book must be a bestseller. Every woman I know feels the need to overcome that worn-out feeling. Every one of us is looking for the bigger answer, the secret key. Anything to teach us how to live this life differently with greater power and energy.

I'm sad to tell you that by the end of the book, I was disappointed. Not necessarily because of the content. I thought the authors did a fabulous job describing worn out in all its various forms. And it's not that they didn't try to help. The writers gave many practical suggestions, things like getting more sleep, forgiving those who have wronged you, living simply, nurturing your friendships, and many other great things we women can do to improve the way we navigate weariness.

It's just that the deep, worn-out ache inside me lingered long past the close of the book. I can only think that your worn-out feeling lingers too. Maybe you have done most of the things experts tell us to do:

- Take your vitamins. *Check.*
- Go on a personal retreat. *Yep. Had several.*
- Simplify your life. *Done that.*
- Cultivate friendships. *Easy, after the "simplify" step left me with two.*
- Get more sleep. *Seven to eight hours every night.*
- Exercise. *Does taking laundry up and down the stairs count?*
- Eat healthy. *Got it, really trying.*
- Organize yourself. *I am a firstborn.*

On and on I could go. At forty-six years old and after following Jesus all these years, I desire a powerful, overcoming life. I want to live like that for God, for my sweet family, and for myself. I hate hitting the wall. I don't want to be worn out or in over my head or always facing more than I can do. The absolute truth of it is that I do everything I can do to battle the fatigue of being on this earth. But tired comes with the gig.

Really, honestly, I believe we can live smarter and make wise choices that improve our circumstances. But when we are obeying God, caring for our families, maintaining our homes, working part-time or full-time, serving at church, and going to soccer games, there is just no way around it: we will become tired, sometimes overwhelmed, and many of us may even live many, many years as worn-out women. (I'm sure that helped you feel encouraged.)

I work really hard all week. Same stuff as you. Lots of laundry. Meals. Car pool. Orthodontist. All the regular mom, wife, and homeowner things you do. Then I travel almost every weekend doing exactly what I believe God has called me to do: meet with women and teach them about Jesus. Usually I get home Saturday night or Sunday morning. For ten years now, I have always thought I can get up on Monday morning and jump right back into my schedule. And every single Monday, I hit the wall.

Yesterday was the Monday after Easter. I didn't travel for ministry. We were all at home. All the children were here, along with Taylor's friends from college. Almost every bed was full and I loved it. We made great meals, cleaned the kitchen a lot, went to church, hung out together, did a little shopping. It was an easy, beautiful family weekend with a Sunday-afternoon nap thrown in as a blessing. I thought I'd be good to go.

But yesterday, Easter Monday, I hit the wall anyway. Exhausted. Fuzzy-headed, I went through the motions of taking a shower and going to my office to work, where I sat in front of my computer and felt like crying most of the day. I was just dog tired, and you know how that makes you want to cry over everything.

After I picked up the kids at school, we came home and I dragged myself upstairs to my bed, snuggled in, and slept for more than an hour. As I drifted off to sleep, I thought, *Good thing I'm working on that chapter about worn out.* Life in all its glory and all its heartache brings fatigue. Physical, emotional, and spiritual. We will all become tired. It's the unavoidable attachment that comes with breathing.

I don't think there is a level of spiritual maturity we can attain that finally catapults us past the propensity to become tired. Exhaustion potential is wired into our humanity. Sometimes people project that a godly woman can overcome being worn out—if only she is organized, living simply and wisely, exercising, and getting enough sleep. An alarm goes off

> We *will all fail if we buy into the idea that we can have a life on this earth that excludes a reccurring weariness.*

inside my head every time a misrepresentation of God sets us up to fail. We will all fail if we buy into the idea that we can have a life on this earth that excludes a reccurring weariness.

Worn out happens.

About the only way I can imagine living without weariness would require my becoming completely self-centered and self-protected. I'd have to block any interruption and stick to my schedule no matter who is offended or who is left out. The whole ridiculous idea seems directly opposed to everything Jesus was about. One of the first instructions He gave to His followers was, "Deny yourself." To deny yourself means you are going to get tired somewhere along the way.

Almost twenty-five years ago, I made an appointment to meet with my beloved seminary professor Dr. Howard Hendricks. I was a second-year student and a grader for his class entitled The Christian Home. Our conversation turned toward my struggles at the time. I was a full-time student and a part-time staff member of a student ministry at a local church. I loved everything I was doing, but I felt stretched and really tired. I think I asked Dr. Hendricks for his keys to balancing the godly life. I was looking for wisdom, a to-do list, anything to get a handle on loving all these people and living this great big life. Dr. Hendricks looked at me so compassionately and said, "Oh, Angela, I still hang myself all the time."

"You do?" I asked, relieved by his truth.

"I do," he said honestly.

Professor Hendricks is one of the greatest men I have ever known. I love that he told me the truth that day and set me free to live wide open, learning along the way how to manage the inevitable "worn-out" feeling that we all will encounter.

I think the spiritual question is, "Where do you go with your worn out? What is your response to the normal fatigue that comes to all of us? And what do you believe about God in the midst of your everyday, run-of-the-mill, exhausted life?"

Here's one thing I am sure of, God knows. He knows that His babygirl is worn out. And so what does our God offer in His Word for me and for you?

We Shall Become Tired

The Bible is so clear on this: we will all become tired, in some way, in some form; and we will all encounter the limitations of our humanity. In other words, every human being will wear out and run down. Each of us has different thresholds of weariness, but none of us is exempt. Scripture gives several observations about our worn-out state:

Work Makes You Tired

I realize that's not big news to those of you who are fighting to keep your sleepy eyes open even as you read this page. But somehow

I take great encouragement in this. Whenever I am dog tired, I remember that the Bible acknowledges throughout its pages that good work makes good people tired. And sometimes when I can barely think one more thought after I lay my head on my pillow, I think to myself, *I am supposed to feel like this when I work hard*. It gives me comfort to remember my design. I am not superhuman. I am only human. I am not supposed to have more than the limits of my physical body. This weakness came with the body, and no one is free from this consequence.

> She has wearied herself with toil.
>
> —EZEKIEL 24:12 (ESV)

Anxious Toil Makes You Even More Tired

In the book of Ecclesiastes, the writer talks about how meaningless life "under the sun" is.

If we don't understand all his references, Solomon could throw us right into a pit of depression with his recurring theme of "Vanity, vanity, it is all vanity." He says that under the sun, everything is meaningless, toil is exhausting, striving is endless. Woven throughout those twelve pounding chapters is the repetitious lesson that "under the sun," it's all meaningless. Perhaps Solomon's words call us to live "with the Son." Where God is. Thinking like God thinks. Doing what God has called us to do. Viewing this life in the light of eternity.

Psalm 127 calls the work we do when we are apart from God's leading *anxious toil*. I am guilty. I bet you are too. We get caught up in aucious toil when we're removed from God's guidance. It's the stuff we strive for "under the sun," that ends up robbing our energy and stealing our joy. Anxious toil will push you over the cliff from exhausted to completely wiped out.

> It is in vain that you rise up early and go late to rest, eating the bread of *anxious toil;* for he gives to his beloved sleep.
>
> —PSALM 127:2 (ESV, italics added)

Just for fun, you have to see what Solomon says about writing books "under the sun." I grin and take this one to heart every time I read it: "Of making many books there is no end, and much study wearies the body" (Ecclesiastes 12:12).

Grief Exhausts the Body and the Soul

We can know great sorrow over our losses, our circumstances, and even our own choices. The soul grieves for many reasons, but the Bible is clear: grief empties us of strength. It will completely wear us out.

> I am worn out from sobbing. All night I flood my bed with weeping, drenching it with my tears. My vision is blurred by grief; my eyes are worn out.
>
> —Psalm 6:6–7 (NLT)

Sin Makes You Tired

Listen to Jeremiah 9:5: "They weary themselves with sinning." How much more clear can it be?

You can wear yourself flat out with sin. Maybe some of you already know that lesson from Scripture. Maybe some of you are living it. Honestly, if you are weary and overwhelmed, this is the very first place I would suggest starting. Are you clean with regard to sin? Blatant things will wear you out, like addictions and adultery, but also check your heart for patterns of gossip and lies— these will wear you out too.

I encountered a woman several years ago who was caught in a web of lies. Almost every interaction with her involved yet another silly lie and stories she had to keep straight. Just ten minutes with her wore me out. I believe that poor woman must have been exhausted from her own sin patterns.

Little choices and small offenses can accumulate in the soul.

You and I have to watch ourselves. Little choices and small offenses can accumulate in the soul. We become burdened with things that don't belong in our lives. Weariness settles in and adds to the everyday fatigue we experience.

Not Like Us, Thankfully

This weekend I spoke in Baton Rouge. We had a great EWomen conference and then last night, my friend Laura and I had a yummy Cajun meal at a local place called Parrin's. (The crawfish étouffée was perfect.) I was happily exhausted and conked out by 9:45. We had a 5 A.M. airport shuttle, so I set my phone alarm for 4 A.M. Six hours of sleep sounded reasonable and enough to get me home.

About 1:30 A.M. the most awful alarm began blaring right inside of my room, and a woman's voice began giving the entire hotel instructions about evacuating. I have no idea how long it took for me to rouse myself from a dead sleep and actually grasp what was happening. Unfortunately, I've had too much experience with middle-of-the-night hotel alarms. Sometimes the all-clear alarm goes off pretty soon, allowing guests to return to their rooms. This one did not. I have learned that I do not want to go outside in my pajamas with all the other guests, so I always change into clothes. And I take my cell phone, purse, jewelry, and room key (you learn the hard way). I pulled myself together and headed down the fire stairs, right out into the pouring rain on a side street.

There I was, standing in mismatched whatever I could find, toting all my worldly goods, dumped out on a side alley in the dark, standing in pouring rain downtown by the Mississippi River, and thinking to myself, *Life just goes like this . . . for everybody.* Plans made. Plans blown through no fault of our own. And in the end, weariness attaches itself to our day and even to our souls.

The fire department came. There was nothing except some rowdy LSU fraternity boys who took it on themselves to invite the entire sold-out hotel to their party. Eventually someone, somewhere figured out how to turn off the screeching alarm inside my room, and a little later they found the switch to turn off the flashing strobe light too. I think I slept twenty more minutes.

I'm writing to you on my second flight this morning. I slept through the first one. I'm more tired than I wanted to be today. But this is the life I have been assigned to, and I'm just a girl who wears out in the normal, human being kind of way.

Thankfully, our God does not. Oh, can I tell you how thankful I am that God in His very nature is so very different from me and you. He does not grow weary. He does not fall asleep or need to be physically replenished. Our God also remembers how we are made. I love Psalm 103:14:

> He knows how we are formed,
> he remembers that we are dust.

Our Creator remembers how He made us. From dust. We can't hold ourselves together. We fall apart. We act like dust that must be squeezed together in the hands of its Creator. God knows how He made me, and that gives me such a deep breath. I am not made divine. I am not superwoman nor will I ever be. I am dust, many days acting like dust. I'm held together by the strong hands of my Lord.

One of the worst things we can do is think about God in terms of familiar human characteristics. God is not some big grandpa in the sky who nods off in his comfy chair. His holy nature is entirely unlike ours. Not only does God not sleep, He does not need to sleep. His character is self-sustaining. He does not need anything from outside Himself to be a better or more powerful God.

I AM Your God Who Does Not Grow Weary

Isaiah makes these promises according to the very nature of our God:

Do you not know?
Have you not heard?
The Lord is the everlasting God,
    the Creator of the ends of the earth.

He will not grow tired or weary,
    and his understanding no one can fathom.
He gives strength to the weary
    and increases the power of the weak.
Even youths grow tired and weary,
    and young men stumble and fall;
    but those who hope in the LORD
    will renew their strength.
They will soar on wings like eagles;
    they will run and not grow weary,
    they will walk and not be faint.

—ISAIAH 40:28–31

Did you read the very clear proclamation of God's character? He will not grow tired or weary. Hallelujah! Now look at how God transfers strength and power to us (the weary): "But *those who hope* in the LORD will renew their strength."

In the next section, we're going to look at God's provisions for the worn out. But this passage contains one of the key ideas for us. This is the part I want to make sure you don't miss: *A hope that is firmly centered on the Lord renews our strength.* In this passage, the word *renew* means "to exchange," like taking off old clothes and putting on new. When we put our hope in God, He is able to exchange our weakness for His power.

Where is your hope today? Most of us know the right answer, but still, it's easy to misplace our hope in the blur of living on this earth. I guess I could fill a journal with all the places I have mistakenly placed my hope. I have hoped in . . .

- Myself or my skill set
- My determination or willpower
- My parents
- My children
- My husband
- My health
- Calm circumstances

- Financial contracts
- The real estate market
- The promises of the well-meaning
- My leaders
- My government

But Isaiah says that those who hope *in the Lord* will renew their strength. Our faith in God ensures a participation in His strength. Other translations say, "those who wait on the Lord, will gain new strength," which is an idea that we see woven throughout Scripture. To put our hope in the Lord is to wait for Him. We'll talk more about this when we discuss God's provisions.

> But those who wait upon God get fresh strength.
> —ISAIAH 40:31 (MESSAGE)

One of the most powerful truths is that our God knows our propensity to become weary. And because *He* does not, we can always trust in His consistent, faithful strength for our souls.

We all think we need a vacation and then realize that a vacation won't be enough. Any woman who has taken a vacation with her family knows that it is just a change of scenery (which helps), but a vacation with children is work, too! A lot of the women I talk to wish they could take a year off from their responsibilities because they feel so helplessly exhausted. Obviously none of us can do that. I believe God has made provisions for our physical, mental, and spiritual selves. Maybe we need to take Him at His word.

God's Provisions for the Worn-Out Woman

As I have been studying this topic these past few weeks, I have grown more and more encouraged about God's provisions for our weariness. As a matter of fact, almost every person I have talked to on the phone the past few days has gotten an earful about how much God understands and cares for His tired baby girls, whether

they wanted to know or not. I am so filled up by these compassionate gifts from God, it's like I'm spilling over on everyone.

True, in this world, we will find ourselves flat worn out, but our
beautiful Father knows our weakness and makes provisions for us.
I am going to list the lessons that have ministered to me. My list is
not exhaustive (pun intended), but hopefully a beginning toward
understanding the heart of God toward the weary.

God's Presence Restores

I don't know how or why God restores us with new energy—
therein lies one of the great mysteries of God—I just know He
does. I think I've known there was something special about the
presence of God since I was little. As a child, when my family
missed church for sickness, travel, and so forth, even then I knew
that something was missing inside of me. I didn't know what it
was, but I think my soul missed being covered with the healing
salve of God's presence.

We are supposed to turn toward the presence of God. Come to
Him. Wait for Him. Look for Him. Jesus said in Matthew 11:28,
"Come to me, all of you who are weary and carry heavy burdens,
and I will give you rest."

The instruction for us is to come. Get to Jesus. Go and find
Him. Be with Him. And the promise is rest—a physical rest for our
weariness and a soul rest from the heavy burdens that weigh on our
minds. Action is required. Are you weary today? Get to Jesus. Run
to Jesus. God promises that His presence renews.

Waiting Often Restores

Over and over in Scripture, we read that the one who is weary drags
himself into the presence of God and waits. We wait for strength.
We wait for guidance. We wait for renewal. In our worn-out days,
I believe that God often longs for us to come into His presence and
then wait for His refreshment.

We wait in hope for the LORD.

—Psalm 33:20

There is a divine mystery in the waiting. God makes a soul transfer in a way I can't understand, but the testimony is clear in Scripture. Maybe our lives with God are supposed to reflect more waiting than rushing. What if, little by little, waiting on God began

> There is a divine mystery in the waiting. God makes a soul transfer in a way I can't understand.

to replace rushing out the door? Your girlfriend calls and asks what you did this afternoon, and you peacefully reply, "I just spent some time waiting on God."

A Sabbath Rest Restores

When I was growing up, my daddy had some very serious rules about Sundays. We were not allowed to work on Sunday. Nada. We didn't mow the yard on Sunday. He wouldn't let me sell Girl Scout cookies on Sunday. No movies. Nothing. We went to church. Had a lunch that my mom had mostly made on Saturday. And then we took a nap that lasted most of the afternoon. When we were old enough, we'd head off to youth group in the evening, then we'd come home, get our things ready for school, and get back into bed. Sunday was mandatory rest for our whole family.

Here's just one example from Scripture about the Sabbath rest: "There remains, then, a Sabbath-rest for the people of God; for anyone who enters God's rest also rests from his own work, just as God did from his" (Hebrews 4:9–10).

> Mr. W. E. Gladstone, the great Victorian statesman, was asked to speak into a phonograph, so that a recording might be made for use fifty years hence. These were the words he spoke: "I owe my life and vigor, through a long and busy life, to the Sabbath day, with its blessed surcease of toil."[1]

As a little girl I assumed that every other family on my street did the same thing we did. That other girls hung up their Sunday dresses after lunch to take afternoon naps in their slips just like me. As a teenager, I found out that no one else was sleeping their

Sunday away. That's about the time I began to think resting on the Sabbath was kind of uncool and probably not necessary.

As a student of the Bible, I am realizing that my dad wasn't too far off. God intended a Sabbath day of rest for His weary created people. He gave the command on purpose, to give honor to Him and to restore our bodies and souls:

> Observe the Sabbath day, to keep it holy.
>
> Work six days and do everything you need to do.
>
> But the seventh day is a Sabbath to God, your God. Don't do any work—not you, nor your son, nor your daughter, nor your servant, nor your maid, nor your animals, not even the foreign guest visiting in your town.
>
> For in six days God made Heaven, Earth, and sea, and everything in them; he rested on the seventh day. Therefore God blessed the Sabbath day; he set it apart as a holy day.
>
> —Exodus 20:8–11 (Message)

What should you and I do on the Sabbath? I think that observing the Sabbath means we should worship the Lord and rest from our work.

I use my mind all week. Moving words around, reading, studying, trying to think about how to communicate an ancient truth in a brand-new way. So walking around in my yard and bending down to pull a few weeds is rest for my mind. It feels like luxurious, frivolous leisure to be in the yard picking up sticks or potting some pansies. Am I breaking the Sabbath? My dad would have said yes and maybe he still feels that way. I say no. If you pull weeds all week for your work, then there is no way that piddling around my backyard would be rest for your soul. I think we have to ask the Lord, "How do I honor You and find rest in this day that You have given us?" Then give yourself permission to obey God.

Even Jesus Required Rest

My second year of seminary, Dr. Martin took me by the shoulders, looked right into my frazzled eyes, and said, "Angela, Jesus did not minister to every person He met. He did not heal everyone who was sick. He did not raise all the dead. He did not go to every town. He only did what His Father instructed Him to do. Just the same, you must only do what God has called you to do. Minister where He leads. Give your heart as He directs." Maybe today, you need to hear my professor's tender words of restraint for your frazzled life, "Only as the Father guides."

Jesus did not minister to every person he met. He did not go to every town. He did only what his Father instructed Him to do.

When God's Son, Jesus, poured Himself into the confines of a human being, He took on all the limitations of our humanity.

> Then Jesus said, "Let's go off by ourselves to a quiet place and rest awhile." He said this because there were so many people coming and going that Jesus and his apostles didn't even have time to eat.
>
> —Mark 6:31 (nlt)

> As often as possible Jesus withdrew to out-of-the-way places for prayer.
>
> —Luke 5:16 (Message)

A pattern of daily and weekly rest should be at the front of our mind-set rather than an afterthought or a prescription from your doctor. We can't keep comparing ourselves to the chaotic world around us. Our ambition is to imitate Christ.

Walking in the Good Way
Provides Rest for Your Soul

Thus says the LORD: Stand by the roads, and look, and ask for the ancient paths, where the good way is; and walk in it, and find *rest* for your souls.

—JEREMIAH 6:16 (ESV, italics added)

Maybe it's old school to talk about being good. It's much more current to be cool or hip or mysteriously aloof. But maybe this old-school idea is full of wisdom. What if we decide to walk in the *good* way? Really. What if, by the power of the Holy Spirit, we surrender to following God's will and choosing the good path. What if we take the good way every time we have a choice? Doing good. Thinking good.

Jeremiah says that every time we choose the path where good is and then walk in it, we find rest for our souls.

Repentance Leads to Refreshing

I hope that you have experienced the freedom and pure delight that comes from being forgiven by God. A great, great joy settles on the forgiven heart. It turns out that repentance is a weariness antidote. To turn away from your sin refreshes the soul: "Repent, then, and turn to God, so that your sins may be wiped out, that times of refreshing may come from the Lord" (Acts 3:19).

To be clean and forgiven gives renewed energy. Sin is blinding, but repentance gives sight. Sin exhausts the mind. Repentance fuels the heart. Sin is toxic for your body and your soul. Repentance removes the poison and brings health to your life.

Godly Friends Refresh Your Soul

Many times, the New Testament writers talked about godly friends who came for a visit and refreshed their souls. Paul wrote that about Stephanas, Fortunatus, and Achaicus: "They have refreshed my spirit and yours. You should recognize the value of people like these" (1 Corinthians 16:18, NCV).

My soul refresher is my friend named Carlye. She has the gift. A few minutes on the phone with her and my heart is refreshed—even though none of my circumstances have changed. I am reminded of how much I am loved. She is always for me. She always has great big hope. And we always laugh our way through the journey.

After my husband, Scott, met Carlye, he said, "I think I'll call her every week. She just has this way of making me feel better." The Apostle Paul said, "You should recognize the value of people like these." In a lifetime, if you make one or two friends who refresh your soul, count yourself among the truly blessed.

And just an extra thought as the Holy Spirit is really convicting me in the moment. Am I a soul refresher? For my husband? My children? The neighbor down the street?

Our Final Rest, Hallelujah!

For years, I've been searching for margins, reconsidering my boundaries, and yearning for an inside soul rest that would make my outside crazy life more peaceful and serene. I am absolutely sure that my soul keeps crying out for its home.

Maybe you are like me, and you long to be free of anxiety. We can't wait to feel amazing all the time. I want to see with clear vision instead of through a sleepy haze. I long for energy to carry out all my heart longs to be. To see more. Give more. Learn and become and change.

Until we get home, to heaven, I take great comfort in believing my heavenly Father knows my worn-out state. He is not frustrated by my weariness. And He has graciously made provisions to minister to my soul. I will refresh the weary and satisfy the faint (Jeremiah 31:25).

My heavenly Father knows my worn-out state. He is not frustrated by my weariness. And He has graciously made provisions to minister to my soul.

One day, we'll step into our final rest. And the woman God dreamed for me and you to be will be realized. When that happens, ask somebody which gold street leads to my house. I want you to come over for dinner. I'll make an amazing meal that took me days. We'll build a fire and dance to great music and stay up all night talking. We'll finally be home. There will be plenty of time. The soul will be free of its weariness. And we will finally be where we belong.

Hallelujah.

Does your heart cry out,
"God, do You know I am worn out?"
Then listen as our Lord speaks to you.
He replies to your worn out heart:

DO YOU KNOW WHO I AM? . . .
I AM your God who does not grow weary.

So, My worn-out daughter, lift up your eyes to the hills to seek your help—your help comes from Me, the One who made you. I AM the Maker of heaven and earth. I AM He, the One who will not let your foot slip—I watch over you, and I will not slumber while you sleep. No, I will neither slumber nor sleep whether you wake or sleep.

I will refresh your tired body and I will restore your tired soul. Come and wait for Me so that I can give you fresh strength. I want you to run and not become weary, walk and not be faint.

Follow the model of My Son, Jesus. Learn to take time for your soul. Wear His yoke, not this world's. Keep a Sabbath day to refresh your body, spirit, and soul.

You are My beloved, and I AM your God who does not grow weary. Forever and ever, amen.[2]

My grace is sufficient for you,
for my power is made perfect in weakness.
—2 CORINTHIANS 12:9

CHAPTER FIVE

DO YOU KNOW I AM SUFFERING WITH A THORN?

He Is My Sufficiency

Every single day there is an ache.

And a million times I have asked the Lord, *Do You know that I'm suffering with a thorn? God, do You know how much this hurts?*

I believe that for a season, perhaps even the rest of my life on this earth, I have been called to suffer a thorn. I pray that you have no idea what I'm talking about. I pray that your calling and your life are thorn-free. But if I know anything about our humanity, I am inclined to think that many of you know the pain of a thorn as well.

Just beginning the words of this chapter immediately made me cry. Sobbing, I write to you that I do not want this thorn.

The Thing About Thorns

I wish with everything inside of me that God would remove this awful plaguing hurt. I am so tired and so very weary of its place in my life. But that is the thing about a thorn. No one wants it. If I could reach down and remove it myself, I would. I have grown to hate its awful torment. And yet, there is absolutely nothing I can do to make it go away. It is a thorn in my flesh until God decides to remove it or until I stand in glory, finally free.

You remember that the apostle Paul wrote in 2 Corinthians 12:

> To keep me from becoming conceited because of these surpassingly great revelations, there was given me *a thorn* in my flesh, a messenger of Satan, to torment me. Three times I pleaded with the Lord to take it away from me. But he said to me, "My grace is sufficient for you, for my power is made perfect in weakness." Therefore I will boast all the more gladly about my weaknesses, so that Christ's power may rest on me. That is why, for Christ's sake, I delight in weaknesses, in insults, in hardships, in persecutions, in difficulties. For when I am weak, then I am strong.
>
> —Verses 7–10

Paul was a great Christ-follower. His life and teachings have guided all the Christ-followers who came after him. A thorn in the flesh of Paul seems noble, something akin to remembering the crown of thorns that Jesus wore at His death. The thorn that Paul spoke of seems apostle-like. I am just a girl from North Carolina. An ordinary Christ-follower. I am nobody compared to Paul. My thorn is not noble. But it is a thorn I am called to bear.

Maybe you realize you have been called to suffer with a thorn as well.

Theologians have long speculated about the nature of Paul's thorn. Most seem to agree that it was some kind of physical afflic-tion, although even in their agreement, no one really knows for sure. Others have speculated that the thorn was an incessant temptation or relentless opponents to his ministry. Somehow, I think it's better that Paul didn't say right out what it was. My thorn involves a relationship that might be

I am just an ordinary Christ-follower. I am nobody compared to Paul. My thorn is not noble. But it is a thorn I am called to bear.

better described as an adversary. And, like Paul, I feel that giving more details of that relationship on this page would be inappropriate. Suffice it to say, there is a thorn.

The Barbs of a Thorn

I cannot speak for Paul, the apostle. I can only speak for me, and I am not an apostle. But I have come to know the barbs of a thorn pretty well by now. Maybe as we talk through the characteristics of a thorn, you will recognize a similar place of suffering in your own life. And if you have been called to suffer a thorn, maybe you will find comfort in these words.

A Thorn Cannot Be Removed by Your Own Power

Three times Paul asked God to remove his thorn, and obviously after three requests the thorn remained. I assume that even though Paul asked God to remove his thorn, he also tried everything in his own strength. If it was a physical ailment, I believe Paul sought treatment. If it was an opponent, I believe Paul tried human intervention and negotiation. But still the thorn remained.

If my own thorn could have been removed by my own strength or if my mind could figure out another way, I am fairly certain that I would have already removed this deep barb. But that is the hallmark of a thorn. No one wants one. The pain is so intense that we avoid the thorn bushes at all costs. And the desire to have it removed is so intense that thorn-bearers would do anything to have it taken away. And yet we cannot, with our own strength, remove what has come to us.

I have fasted, prayed, sought counsel, screamed, felt sorry for myself, and prayed all over again. Year after year goes by, and the unwanted truth is that I cannot remove this thorn. People look at me with sad eyes and say, "I am so sorry this is your thorn to bear." But there is nothing they can do. Many have tried. The thorn is so deep. I have come to believe that it is my thorn to bear and yet not mine to remove. It is God's to remove—in His timing, whether in this life or the life to come. God is *El Shaddai,* God Almighty, the God who can do anything He chooses.

The Originator of the Thorn Is Satan

I don't see demons, at least not normally. I have been with people who talk about seeing demons all the time. Or they theorize that demons are behind almost everything that goes wrong. A squeak in the sound system—demon. A delayed flight—demon. The flu bug—you guessed it—a demon.

Year after year goes by, and the unwanted truth is that I cannot remove this thorn.

I don't see demons so much, but I believe in them. I think they are actively at work, but I also believe that we live in a fallen world where people make mistakes. And even really good people do dumb things that result in negative consequences that we all have to bear. So I don't think every bad thing or every inconvenience is the work of a demon. We certainly do enough to ourselves.

But if there is anything I know for certain about my thorn, I know that it comes from the evil one and that its place in my life is purposed for evil. The apostle Paul wrote that his thorn was a messenger from Satan. I believe all such thorns originate in the mind of Satan. He is the one who orchestrates their placement and their pain. And maybe, according to the hierarchy of his dark world, he sends demons to push on the thorns that have been acutely placed in our fleshly places.

Satan is the author of evil. He is the rival of God, and everything he does works against the kingdom of God. He brings affliction and perversion. He wants people to miss the truth of eternity. He brings sickness, loneliness, financial loss, devastating circumstances, and hurtful relationships that cannot seem to be undone. I know that he is the giver of thorns.

I was picking up my son Grayson from a summer afternoon football practice. It had been miserably hot that day. The kids had been running and drinking a lot of Gatorade. About half of them had gotten sick from the combination. One of the coaches, who is a friend, came over to my car in the pickup line. He joked with me about the tough practice. "They don't have to preach to me about hell, I have been there." It had been a grueling thorn day for me and I thought to myself, *They don't have to preach to me about the devil either; I have talked to him on the phone.*

I believe Satan purposes every thorn for evil. He wants to hurt you, discourage you, and tell you lies. He wants you to doubt yourself and doubt God, which leads us to the next barb of a thorn. Satan is mean.

A Thorn Torments the Soul with Pain and Doubt

If there is a question associated with a thorn, that question has to be, "Why?" I have searched my own heart and life so many times. A prolonged day-after-day thorn can begin to make you doubt your own worth. And some days you wonder, "Do I deserve this somehow? Have I caused this pain? Is this a consequence of some mistake I made or sin I committed?"

The answers are always no. I know God. I know the depth of His love for sinners and the heart of His goodness toward the ones that He loves. A thorn may be allowed by God and God may turn what was meant for evil into good. But a thorn is not given by God for punishment. The thorn is from Satan for the purpose of evil. It is the ongoing pain that plants the doubts. The uninformed words of others can fuel your doubt. But we have to settle the truth in our hearts. Satan wants us to doubt God. The thorn is one means of making us doubt.

A Thorn Pierces Your Heart with Discouragement

We are called to live passionate lives for Jesus Christ. Imitating Him. Multiplying our gifts. Serving. Giving. Loving. Growing in maturity. Seeing eternity. Living sacrificial God-centered lives. Which all sounded really great when you were away at youth camp, singing "pass-it-on" around a camp fire, throwing the stick representing your sin into the flames to be burnt for all eternity.

But here we are in the real world where youth camp is a distant memory that seems like it happened to someone else. Most of us plod along with financial difficulties, family issues, or some minor health concerns. A passionate life is difficult enough without the discouragement a thorn can weave into your calling.

I have even said, "Maybe Satan would leave me alone if I settled for a mediocre life or dial back my calling."

In some of my most discouraged moments I have even said out loud, "Maybe Satan would leave me alone if I settled for a mediocre life or dial back my calling." You know what, maybe he would.

I cannot even pretend to know the mind of such meanness. All I know is that the unrelenting thorn can be discouraging. And we can begin to question ourselves and what we thought God put us on the planet for and why any of it matters.

The Piercing of a Thorn Produces Weakness

I think one of Satan's best tactics is observation. He doesn't have many new ideas, but he watches and he pays attention to our hearts. He watches and decides to place a thorn where it will produce a weakness. But here is the irony: Over time, because of God's tenderness, the endured weakness can become a strength.

My thorn has made me weak in so many areas. I spent years doubting my own intelligence and ability to make wise decisions because of my thorn. I came to believe I was gullible or naive without a strong spiritual discernment. I lived in such intense fear. Fear of the thorn. Even afraid that the thorn would rip apart my entire life, ministry, and future. From that fear, I lived in weakness, like the weak-willed woman in 2 Timothy 3 who were easy targets for those who would "worm their way in": "They are the kind who worm their way into homes and gain control over weak-willed women" (2 Timothy 3:6).

Maybe your thorn has produced a weakness in you. Maybe your struggles are physical, but so often even our physical weakness becomes an emotional battle. Fought on the inside. Easily hidden from sight. A private weakness where Satan has stuck his pointed thorn.

God Decides When to Remove a Thorn

Paul asked God three times to remove his thorn. I am sure that Paul asked God to remove his thorn because he knew it would not come out any other way. If it were possible to free ourselves from a daily torture, I think most of us would set ourselves free. But a thorn can only be removed by God. In His time. In His way.

As far as we know, the apostle carried his thorn to his death. But I do not believe that all thorns remain for a lifetime. God decides when. It seems that some are endured for a season. And some are not taken out until heaven. My friend Jan Silvious said to me a couple of months ago, "Angela, God lets you get to peaceful waters." I told her that I don't know what that's like. She said, "God can give a peacefulness in His time."

I imagine that to have a thorn removed must be to the soul like the morning after the flu has passed. The relief it must bring. The awfulness is gone. Or maybe it's like the moment after a splinter is removed and you can take a deep, long breath again. Except there will be day after day of deep breaths, a quiet inner rejoicing over the freedom of relief from pain.

Humility

We were splitting a plate of spaghetti in a restaurant in Colorado even though I had met the woman I was having dinner with only that day. Women are kind of like that. "Wanna share something?" But this woman was especially like that. She was safe and her heart was warm. She was the kind of woman you'd want to have as a friend. She was also a Christian counselor with a long list of psychology degrees and accomplishments. She was very smart, but there was something more than that. She was gracious. Peaceful. Interested.

The conversation began with the usual for both of us. Tell me about your family. Your ministry. We traded descriptions and pictures and travel schedules. It felt like I had stumbled onto a kindred spirit. Then in her safe way, the Christian counselor began to pry. You know—the insider questions that you don't usually answer for just everybody.

The Constant Nature of Thorns

Eventually we tripped across my thorn. Sticking out there plain as day for this discerning woman to see. But I am so tired of my thorn.

And embarrassed by it. This story is old and I cannot stand to hear the words coming out of my mouth anymore. Just flat exhausted by its constant poking. The counselor could tell. Maybe my tears were a dead give-away. Tired thorn tears.

It's Okay to Hate Your Thorn
She said exactly what any great thinking woman who loves God would say. "I hate your thorn."

"I hate it too," I said, meaning it.

"Angela, the thorn keeps you humble," she wisely observed.

"I don't want to be humble anymore. I'm tired of being embarrassed. I'm tired of the constant pain. I'm tired of being ashamed. What if I try arrogant for a while?"

She laughed.

I laughed too. I didn't mean it, but years of a thorn can make you consider the options.

Paul, the Christ-follower, said that his thorn kept him from becoming conceited (2 Corinthians 12:7). Still, he asked for it to be removed, hoping, I guess, that he could battle the possibility of conceit by sheer determination. I feel the same way about humility. I have promised God that I would live such a grateful life without my thorn. I would determine never to become arrogant or conceited or self-righteous. I will never forget what it feels like to live like this. And yet, the thorn remains.

So what will a thorn teach me about humility?

Brokenness and embarrassment and the mean attacks from Satan happen to other people all the time. The lessons from my thorn keep me connected to people at the very heart of their pain and doubt.

> *The lessons from my thorn keep me connected to people at the very heart of their pain and doubt.*

To be humble means to "be relatively low in rank and without pretensions." Humility keeps me aware of my position. Pretension stays far away.

It seems like there are hundreds of women without thorns who could do what I do and be better at it without the distraction. So I am grateful that God calls me anyway. And uses me in ways that are amazing and powerful.

I had hoped that humility would be a part of my character as a by-product of spiritual maturity. And maybe it is. Maybe maturity is the means by which the lessons of the thorn are learned and applied.

How Long, Oh Lord

A couple of months ago, some people from my church met with me for prayer. As usual, we prayed for the thorn to be removed. We asked God to relieve me and my children from this pain. We asked for healing from these wounds. We just asked God to make it stop.

And then I prayed, "How long, oh Lord? How long must this endure?" No one in the room had an answer. Nothing. All we know is that the thorn will remain until God decides it is enough. Obviously, at least three times, Paul thought his suffering had lasted long enough. And so he prayed three times. Job suffered miserably until God intervened. Jesus asked His Father if the suffering on the cross could pass from Him. Our humanity rightfully cries out, "How long, Lord? Is this enough now? Will You end the pain?"

Here is where our faith must intersect the mystery of God with trust. No one knows the mind of God (Isaiah 55:8). His ways are not our ways and His thoughts are not our thoughts. I am not divine, only flesh. I am not all-seeing, just narrowly focused on myself and the ones I love. And so my commitment to Christ requires me to trust.

"How long" belongs to the mind of God. I must remember what I know of His character. He is my Creator. He has loved me since before my first breath. He has pursued me and called me to follow Him with my life. Through His Son, Jesus, He has saved me from punishment and set me apart for all eternity. He will safeguard my heart and decide how long my thorn will remain.

I need to remember that God's grace is sufficient. He is enough for all that I face. He is enough for you too.

I AM Your God Who Is Sufficient

When Paul asked God to remove his thorn, the Lord responded with some of the most amazing words in Scripture:

> But he said to me, "My grace is sufficient for you, for my power is made perfect in weakness."
>
> —2 Corinthians 12:9

The tense of the verb Paul uses allows us to read the beginning of the passage this way, "And God has once-for-all said to me." Paul meant for us to understand that God's response to him was the final answer on the issue of his thorn. The dictionary says that *sufficient* means "enough to meet the needs of a situation." God is sufficient. His decisions. His timing. His motives. His grace. God did not give Paul an explanation, He gave him a promise from His character. We are called to live on the promises of God.

It is only God who could perfect His power inside the weakness that a thorn brings. But here is the most beautiful part of God's sufficiency: it doesn't just get us through—it transforms! Paul lived in victory not because God took away his thorn, but because God's power came to his life in the weakness.

I'll tell you what this passage has come to mean to me. I am learning that these circumstances may never change. Their intensity could actually increase and the pain may never fade. This thorn could last one more day or perhaps it will last for the rest of my life. The various briars and patches of more thorns may not end either. But God Himself will give a grace, and then a new grace, to walk through every day.

> Not that we are sufficient of ourselves to think any thing as of ourselves; but our sufficiency is of God.
>
> —2 Corinthians 3:5 (KJV)

God is sufficient and that means He is enough. He is actively involved in my life and therefore He is transferring His sufficiency to me for every situation. Today. I am breathing in and out. He is enough. My soul is at peace. Read Paul's words about the sufficiency of God's grace: "And God is able to make all grace abound to you, so that in all things at all times, having all that you need, you will abound in every good work" (2 Corinthians 9:8). Maybe we could just say it all together . . . God is, in *all* things, at *all* times, *all* that I need. All means all, and not sort of all. Bless the Lord, He gives all that we need.

The sufficiency of God means that I can still live a passionate life, even with this thorn in my side with its ever-present ache. It means that somewhere along the way, I laid down my anger. Or maybe the circumstances taught me that anger held no value. Either way, the weirdest gift is to hurt so bad and not rage on the inside with anger. That has to be God's sufficiency.

Sufficient grace means that I am not the free, funny, goof-around mom that I thought I was going to be, but I am enough of that to enjoy.

Sufficient grace means that as tired as I am of this thorn, deep inside of me is a determination not to let Satan win.

Sufficient grace means that my weakness will become the backdrop for God's power. And so my weakness must be known, in order for God's glory to be seen. And there is great humility in showing my weakness.

Made Perfect in Weakness

> Therefore I will boast all the more gladly about my weaknesses, so that Christ's power may rest on me. That is why, for Christ's sake, I delight in weaknesses, in insults, in hardships, in persecutions, in difficulties. For when I am weak, then I am strong.
>
> —2 Corinthians 12:9–10

Wow. Some truly amazing things are happening in Paul's heart. He asked God to remove his thorn and three times God refused. But when Paul allowed himself to be transformed by our God who is sufficient, two amazing things happened:

1. Paul boasts about his weakness and then the power of Christ comes to rest on him.
2. Paul delights in his weakness and then strength is transferred to him.

I want that. All of it. I want the sufficiency of God in my heart and in my home, my marriage, my parenting, and my ministry. I want what happens when a thorn causes us to know God as sufficient and enough. I truly want God's power and strength. I had just forgotten that God uses thorns to shape hearts and lives for His glory.

> The last and greatest lesson that the soul has to learn is the fact that God, and God alone, is enough for all its needs. This is the lesson that all His dealings with us are meant to teach; and this is the crowning discovery of our whole Christian life. *God is enough!*[1]
>
> —HANNAH WHITALL SMITH

At the end of these thoughts is the one big truth: My life isn't about me. It is supposed to be about one woman's lifetime spent bringing glory to the God of Wonders. And He receives the glory in my weakness. Amazing.

Does your heart cry out,
"God, do You know I am suffering with a thorn?"
Then listen as our Lord speaks to you.
God replies to your suffering heart:

DO YOU KNOW WHO I AM? . . .
I AM sufficient.

I AM able to meet all of your needs according to my abundant riches. I will give you enough grace for your thorn. I AM able. Able to make grace abound, able to give all that you need, able to manage all things.

I made the heavens and the earth with My outstretched arm. Nothing is too hard for me. I AM strong and mighty. I AM great and abundant in strength. All power belongs to Me. I want you to know I AM able to do anything. I want you to know that everything I have promised to you, I AM fully able to do.

In your own power and in your own strength, it may be impossible for you to manage, but not with Me. All things are possible with Me. So believe. Believe in Me, My beloved.

You are Mine. I AM your God who is sufficient for all you need. Forever and ever, amen. [2]

*If we confess our sins, he is faithful and just
and will forgive us our sins and
purify us from all unrighteousness.*
—1 JOHN 1:9

CHAPTER SIX

DO YOU KNOW
I AM A SINNER?

He Is My Savior

I am having an affair."

A woman I had never met was standing in front of me, choking on the pain of her sin. She had come to ask me to pray for her. Her words were barely audible through her sobs. My heart broke as I leaned in to hold her and to listen. We sat together on a pew inside an empty sanctuary, and it was awhile before she was able to continue.

> Keep vigilant watch over your heart;
> 　　that's where life starts.
> Don't talk out of both sides of your mouth;
> 　　avoid careless banter, white lies, and gossip.
> Keep your eyes straight ahead;
> 　　ignore all sideshow distractions.
> Watch your step,
> 　　and the road will stretch out smooth before you.
> Look neither right nor left;
> 　　leave evil in the dust.
>
> —PROVERBS 4:23–27 (MESSAGE)

When the young brunette woman was finally able to speak, there was more truth than I had imagined, and then it just continued to get worse. She told me that she was having her second affair in this marriage. She had been caught in the first affair and had begged her husband to go with her to counseling. He had forgiven her and taken her back, and their marriage had been restored. They had a baby girl, now almost two years old. She said that she loved her husband very much. But now she was involved in another affair that had been going on for almost a year. This affair was still hidden from her husband. And then she told me the worst part of her confession—she did not want the affair to end.

She went on to tell me how much she loved God and wanted to serve Christ. She talked about her baby girl and her marriage. But the truth that kept her in bondage was her honest admission. She did not want to stop blatantly sinning in the face of God and in the face of her husband.

> But if serving the LORD seems undesirable to you, then
> choose for yourselves this day whom you will serve, whether
> the gods your forefathers served beyond the River, or the
> gods of the Amorites, in whose land you are living. But as
> for me and my household, we will serve the LORD.
> —JOSHUA 24:15

There is just no way to follow Christ and choose to remain in your sin. The woman who is called to follow Jesus Christ is also called to run—and I mean run for her life—away from her sin.

When a Good Girl Chooses Sin

As you can imagine, my discussion with this woman lasted for a while. I only heard pieces of her thirty-eight years. I can't remember her name, but her face and her turmoil are etched in my mind. She has chosen sin, and any one of us is not above choosing the same. Maybe you believe you would never choose to have an affair. Maybe not. But none of us is exempt from the allure of sin. The choices may be different. The enticements vary. The sin that captures you may be nothing like having an affair, but sin is sin is sin. The Bible says we have all sinned. With great

> *Maybe you believe you would never choose to have an affair. Maybe not. But none of us is exempt from the allure of sin.*

awareness of our humanity, we can turn to God and ask, "Oh God, do You know that I am a sinner?"

Sin is disobedience to God. Sin is a turning away from His teaching. Choosing sin is like bowing down at the altar you have built for yourself. If there is sin in your life, something dies in its presence. Being free of sin gives life and all its blessing.

Do you remember the promise of Deuteronomy?

> I command you today to love the LORD your God, to walk in
> his ways, and to keep his commands, decrees and laws; *then*
> *you will live and increase, and the* LORD *your God will bless*
> *you. . . .*
>
> But if your heart turns away and you are not obedient, and
> if you are drawn away to bow down to other gods and wor-
> ship them, I declare to you this day that you will certainly be
> destroyed. . . .
>
> This day I call heaven and earth as witnesses against
> you that I have set before you life and death, blessings and
> curses. Now *choose life,* so that you and your children may
> live and that you may love the Lord your God, listen to his
> voice, and hold fast to him. For the Lord is your life.
>
> —30:16–20 (italics added)

I have in mind the woman I counseled with. But let's just think for a moment. How does such blatant and sneaky sin happen to a Christ-follower? A woman like her, or a woman like me or you? Maybe it goes something like this:

A Young Girl Asks Jesus Christ to Be Her Savior

Do you remember the great, great joy of that moment? Knowing for sure that your sins have been forgiven and your eternity is certain. Feeling so much hope and promise. I remember the peace that came to me when I finally understood that Jesus wanted me, just me. That God's forgiveness lasts forever. That nothing can remove my salvation or disown me as a child of God. I was taken in by such a deep and abiding peace. A peace that gives life meaning and makes the everyday-ness of life full of purpose and fun.

I remember making the decision in college to surrender my life fully to God. I wanted to know Him and follow His teachings. I wanted to imitate Christ and live full of His purpose. I imagine that you remember coming to know Jesus as your Savior, but if you cannot, return to chapter 2 and read about being saved.

I think most of us begin well. At least in the moments surrounding our coming to Christ, the heart is pure and the desire to follow God is strong and purposeful. The sweetness of this decision and commitment can last for a lifetime, carrying you year after year into the next step of your walk with God. But for some, the memory of God's goodness and the decision to follow can begin to fade. I think that is where the opportunity to choose sin begins.

She Forgets

My children have attended a Christian school since kindergarten. They have attended church almost every Sunday of their lives and, for many years, Sunday and Wednesday nights as well. Every one of them participates in youth group, Bible studies, mission trips, and anything else the youth pastor can think of, not to mention Young Life and all its great programs.

On top of all that, their mom works for Jesus. Many weekends are like this past weekend. I took the kids out of school early and loaded up the car for a women's conference and our spring break trip all rolled into one. We drove to a beautiful church in Eden, North Carolina, and met about five hundred women for their spring women's weekend. The kids carried boxes of books, sat in the worship center, and sang along with the worship band, listened to their mom speak for what must seem like the umpteenth time, and watched as women came to the altar, cried, and prayed. We went back to our hotel room and got up the next morning for a full Saturday at the women's conference with me speaking a couple of times, more worship, and more tender stories from the hearts of women. When the conference was over, we were off to the mountains for spring break, happy about the weekend with the women, almost dancing over the four who prayed to receive Christ, and looking forward to a week of snow.

To say that my kids are exposed to the truths of Jesus would be a ridiculous understatement. They are saturated and sopping. And here is my concern: that they would forget; that their surroundings would become so familiar that they would begin to take for granted

> *You and I could simply forget how good God has been to us. May it never be.*

what is really happening all around them. The powerful presence of God is changing lives and glorifying Himself, and somehow in the daze of having seen it all, they could cease to be amazed.

A woman can forget about the riches she has received because she has grown accustomed to their presence. Or a woman can forget about God's goodness because she turns the intent of her heart. You and I, we could just forget how good God has been to us. May it never be.

She Allows Herself One Taste

When I was growing up, my daddy always used to tell me that no one ever intends to become an alcoholic, but you cannot become an alcoholic if you never take the first taste. His words kept me from even taking the tiniest taste of anything alcoholic all through college and well into my late thirties. Would I have become an alcoholic if I had tasted a beer? No, I don't think so. But I also believe my dad. There was one way to be sure. Don't begin.

I think that principle holds for other choices as well. No gambling addiction without the first bet. No cocaine trap without the first snort. No illicit sex without the first illicit partner. Every addiction finds its truth in this pattern. You will not become the town gossip without the first whisper. No tax evasion without the first cheat. I think you see how this goes.

One day, the woman who has surrendered her heart and her life to follow Christ can grow numb to the glory of God and allow herself one little indulgence. One taste of what has been forbidden. Of course, the woman who has sinned can run to her Savior with the truth of her choice. Receive forgiveness. Be made clean. And run away from her sin. But for many, the one taste is the beginning they live to regret. To allow a taste of what has sin potential is to play with the wellness of your soul.

I knew a mom whose godly teenage daughter, Sasha, decided to get drunk one night. A friend made Sasha a potent mix of vodka and Gatorade. It was the first time she had ever tasted alcohol. The young girl made herself so sick that night that she vowed to her mom and all of her friends that she would never, ever drink alcohol again. The mom was sad but relieved. She told me, "Maybe she's learned her lesson." I'm sure you know where this goes. A few months later the mom received a phone call. A concerned neighbor called to say that all the kids were concerned about Sasha's frequent and secret drinking. One decision to taste. One taste with so many consequences, and now so much broken trust and pain.

She Learns to Live Around the Consequences

I'm sure the woman who was having an affair just figured out how to live with the consequences of her cheating. She taught her mind to grow numb to the guilt of every lie she told. She looked into her husband's eyes and chose not to see his heart. She kept her emotions focused on herself and her misplaced lust. She placed her own desire above God's commandment. I don't know the past years of her life, but I am sure so much of her pain could be traced back to the choice to choose sin's death over the clean life God has called us to.

I had a professor in seminary, Dr. Norman Geisler, who is perhaps one of the most brilliant men on the planet. In one of our apologetics classes, he said to us, "If I ever feel myself coming down with something, the very first thing I do is check my heart to see if there is any unconfessed sin." Dr. Geisler went on to say that he might just be getting sick; sometimes we just get sick. But he did not want to bring any sickness into his life because of the presence of sin. Ever since that class, I have found myself doing the same thing. Amazingly, sometimes I have confessed my sin and spent a powerful time with God, to find that later my sore throat or achy body recovers. Many times I confess my sin and still come down with the flu. I may get sick from time to time, but I certainly don't want sin and its darkness to make me unhealthy.

I don't have any scientific proof on this connection. No big studies. But I do believe that hidden sin and all its consequences can make people sick. So much stress is associated with living an unclean life, I don't want anything to do with it. And here's the thing about consequences—you can live around them for years, maybe even incorporate the consequences into your normal life. But I know for sure that consequences catch up with you. Maybe not soon enough, but eventually. My word to the woman choosing to sin against God, thinking she is managing her consequences pretty well: Girl, you'd better duck, because it will all come undone and the cost will be more than you could have imagined.

She Accepts a New Normal

Hiding her sin and keeping track of the lies becomes a new normal for the woman who is choosing to live in the presence and practice of sin. What once looked repulsive and unwanted is now accepted and even embraced. The woman who used to long after God resigns herself to less than God's promised life. She manages her conse-

> *The woman who used to long after God now manages the consequences of her sin.*

quences. Lives far from God. Keeps her eyes on herself.

Maybe you are not living the blatant sin of an affair, but you know there is sin in your life that has become your "normal." Let your soul pray this question to your heavenly Father, "Oh God, do You know that I am a sinner?"

May It Never Be

Let's look together at what the Bible says. Paul writes to the believers in Rome:

> What shall we say then? Are we to continue in sin so that grace
> may increase? *May it never be!*
>
> —ROMANS 6:1–2 (NASB, italics added)

When I was in seminary, we had to memorize the entire chapter of Romans 6. I'm not sure if I understood why at the time, but all these years later, I get it. Sin and its varied enticements are ever present. The sin potential within our hearts will never diminish, nor will it be removed until we are finally free of it in heaven. But, as believers, we have to mature into the strength of our calling. We cannot choose sin or keep sinning or remain in the presence of sin. May it never be!

In verse 1 of Romans 6, Paul asks the question, "Are we to continue in sin so that grace may increase?" He then answers his own question in verse 2 with one of his favorite exclamations, "May it never be!" Essentially, he's saying, "No way, José!" And the Greek word (*me genoito*) is even more impressive. My Romans Bible professor explained to us that if Paul could have stacked a hundred football fields end-to-end and as high and as far as those fields could reach, that would be the enormousness of his intent. I imagine that he would yell to each one of us, "Listen to me, may it never be! A hundred football fields high, never be!"

We just cannot choose sin. Verse 13 of Romans 6 says that instead, we are supposed to present our bodies as instruments of righteousness. Paul says that Jesus Christ has given us a new life. Our calling is to live that new life according to His will and empowered by the Holy Spirit who now lives within us. I love *The Message* paraphrase here:

> That means you must not give sin a vote in the way you conduct
> your lives. Don't give it the time of day. Don't even run little
> errands that are connected with that old way of life. Throw

yourselves wholeheartedly and full-time—remember, you've been raised from the dead!—into God's way of doing things. Sin can't tell you how to live. After all, you're not living under that old tyranny any longer. You're living in the freedom of God.

verses 12–14

Running away from sin means that you and I will have to act like the One we belong to. We have to think and respond and sometimes do the hardest thing for one reason only—we are Christ-followers, called to live righteous lives.

Do you keep on sinning when you have been set free from sin's bondage by our Savior? May it never be!

I AM Your God Who Saves You

We have a way out of this whole mess! Hallelujah, we really do. God saves us, through Jesus, for all eternity. Maybe the most beautiful attribute of God is that He is our Savior. He shows an infinite grace toward each one of us so that our lives can be redeemed of sin. He saves us from the bondage of sin on this earth through our relationship with Him, by the power of the Holy Spirit.

I, even I, am the LORD, and apart from me there is no savior.

—ISAIAH 43:11

We do not have to live with soul-wearying sin in our lives. God has made a way out. He says to us, "Do you know who I AM? I AM your Savior." God has made a way for us to live, running away from our sin and running toward the freedom our Savior gives.

God Has Made a Way for Us to Run
from Sin and Toward the God Who Saves

Yesterday I was talking to a different Christian woman after a different conference. One thing that she said really stuck with me as she told me about the choices she was making in her life. I asked why she hadn't left her sin, chosen a higher path, or done things differently by now? Why hadn't she turned toward her Savior and run away from her sin? She looked at me with tears in her eyes, her empty stare making me feel like she was lost, and then she said, "I don't know how." My heart broke for her. So, as urgently as I can, I want to tell you how the Bible says to run away from your sin.

Don't Wait for a Wake-up Call

Time after time you will hear someone say, "I knew what I was doing was wrong, but then so-and-so happened and it was a real wake-up call for me." Good grief. Always, and I mean always, the wake-up call is something terrible. Please don't wait for some real-life tragedy or consequence to jolt you from your sin stupor. Hear God calling you today. Run away from your sin. Don't wait to be motivated. Just decide to obey.

> But there's also this, it's not too late—God's personal Message!—
> "Come back to me and really mean it! Come fasting and weep-
> ing, sorry for your sins!" Change your life, not just your clothes.
> Come back to God, *your* God. And here's why: God is kind
> and merciful. He takes a deep breath, puts up with a lot, this
> most patient God, extravagant in love, always ready to cancel
> catastrophe.
>
> —JOEL 2:12–13 (MESSAGE)

Deny Yourself

A few days ago, a woman said, "I will try to stay away from my sin." I felt my heart sink because of her lack of resolve. Running away from sin requires a dogged determination, something a hundred times more serious than a "try." Peter was a devoted follower of Jesus, but several times, Jesus had to correct Peter's focus. Just like me and you, Peter was inclined to focus on himself. Many times his pride and his choices kept him from a powerful walk with the Lord.

Here's the thing about denying yourself: It hurts. You do not let yourself have what you desire and you will feel an ache like a tearing when you tell yourself no. Yesterday my friend Carlye and I went to a great Mexican restaurant in Fort Worth. Carlye and I are seriously on a get-crazy-healthy diet. We are in the weight-loss phase, both of us wanting to reach our goals. There we were at a Mexican restaurant ordering two salads with salsa and two Diet Cokes. But the server came with a beautiful bowl of chips, our absolute favorite thing in the whole wide world. I mean, we are both self-proclaimed connoisseurs of chips and guacamole coast-to-coast. But chips are not allowed during our goal-weight diet. So we looked at them. And talked about how great they probably tasted. And made a plan to come back to that restaurant when chips are allowed again. And prayed for an abundance of chips in heaven. But neither one of us had a bite. We denied ourselves. Honestly, the salad was fine, but not eating the chips was painful.

To deny yourself is not going to be fun. At least in the beginning, denial will be painful. Actually, it might take away what you have come to regard as fun, and you will have to redefine what gives you pleasure. That's the thing about sin, it can be pleasurable for a moment and in the end, lead to death. I imagine that having those chips would have given Carlye and me a great amount of lunchtime pleasure, but in the end would, kill the bigger dream of a healthier body.

> Then he said to them all: "If anyone would come after me, he must deny himself and take up his cross daily and follow me."
>
> —Luke 9:23

I realize that denying ourselves a bowl of chips does not come even close to the depth of a sin problem. I hear some of you saying, "Angela, my sin is so much bigger than a bowl of chips." I believe you. My sin has been bigger than a bowl of chips too. So, since this one thought is the place where we most often fail, I want to spell it out for you with a few bolder examples:

- If a man who is not your husband hugs you longer than you both know is appropriate, do not return his embrace. Do not allow yourself any comfort there. Even if everything inside of you desires to be held, you must deny yourself completely. If you have ADD (Affection Deficit Disorder), this one will be so very tempting. And the denial of affection will rip at your longing.

- Even if your day has been a complete disaster, no one on the planet understands, and you'd rather forget all your troubles, you cannot give in to any form of destructive addiction or behavior. You cannot get drunk. You cannot get high or check out or choose any kind of sin to distract you from your heartache. To deny yourself an escape means you stay in the pain and it hurts. It can really, really hurt to focus on your life instead of running from it.

- You are standing at the end of the driveway talking to your neighbors. You enjoy the banter and the company, but the conversation turns into gossip about a mutual friend. You just happen to know the scoop, and it would be enjoyable to tell what you know. But you cannot. You must deny yourself the pleasure of being heard.

The point about denial is that whatever is denial for you will be tough until it becomes habit and then eventually becomes character. Your temptations will not be mine and mine will not be yours. But I think you know when you are about to choose sin. So deny yourself. Cry about it if you have to. Stomp your feet. Say you want the sin. Tell God you want to sin. Then deny yourself anyway.

Hightail It Away

Turn away. Get away. Run as fast as you can in the opposite direction of the sin that promises to consume you. I hope that somehow you can read these words with the intensity with which I am writing them. You have to run, not walk. Sprint, not sashay. Determine, not dawdle. You just cannot hang out anywhere near your sin triggers. Remember how Joseph dealt with the temptation of Potiphar's wife:

She pestered him day after day after day, but he stood his ground. He refused to go to bed with her. On one of these days he came to the house to do his work and none of the household servants happened to be there. She grabbed him by his cloak, saying, "Sleep with me!" He left his coat in her hand and ran out of the house.

Genesis 39:10–12 (Message)

If a certain friend has a way of bending your resolve, then you cannot be with her. If a boyfriend has helped you lower your standards, then call him today and tell him it's over. If your loneliness tempts you to fall, then you will have to stay very busy and, by whatever means, cut loneliness from your day. To get away from sin will probably mean some kind of physical decision about what you look at, what you buy, where you go, and who you are with.

Figure out how to live your life differently. Don't keep driving down the same road where the same temptations hang out. Take another way home.

Say a quiet *yes* to God and he'll be there in no time. Quit dabbling in sin. Purify your inner life. Quit playing the field.

—James 4:8 (Message)

Stay Away

Chain yourself to a wall far, far away from your sin. Here is one thing I know: when we have a purpose on this earth, whether it be family or ministry or a great job that we love, and we want to live that purpose with passion and integrity, sin becomes a lot less enticing. So, in effect, the best way I know to stay away from your sin is to get an amazing life. Go help some people or do something that matters. Gather up some toiletries and snacks and put them in a bag, get in your car, and drive back to the homeless woman you passed on the corner this morning. Do something with your life that keeps you chained to God's purpose instead of your sin.

Celebrate Choosing Right!
It's a big, big deal to do the right thing, especially if the wrong thing has been kicking you for a long time. So whoop it up! Have some friends over. Give yourself a celebratory hour off. Take a walk, read a book. Stop and thank God for His power inside of you!

Ignoring God

I see it all around me every day. People who say they follow Jesus with their mouths but who ignore the Savior with their lives. I also watch, even now, some friends who seem to get away with it. They live in secret sin, life goes along, and many look like they are living without consequences. But what I know about God is that He will not be ignored, nor will He be mocked by people who pretend to be His followers. Paul writes, "Do not be deceived: God cannot be mocked. A man reaps what he sows" (Galatians 6:7).

Sin deceives you into thinking that the instructions of God can be ignored. That maybe you'll skim by anyway. Here is one thing I have witnessed about the character of God: He may give you time to return to Him, but He will not let you keep on trying to make a fool of Him. A woman I know distantly just got caught in an affair that has been going on for ten years. I think she had begun to believe she could get away with it forever. But what you do in the dark will come back to you. It's the law of God. It's a reckless game to think you can get away with ignoring the One who loves you endlessly.

When I was a little girl and I'd hear someone say, "God will not be mocked," it would make my knees feel weak. To think about intentionally daring to mock God scared the spit out of me. Now that I am a grown woman and I have seen the consequences of choosing sin in the face of God, my knees still go weak, my stomach goes queasy, and my throat begins to swell.

> *God may give you time to return to Him, but He will not let you keep on trying to make a fool of Him.*

You are free to sin if you are willing to eventually pay everything. But a godly woman cannot ignore our God who wants us to know Him as Savior. The bondage breaker. The forgiver of our sins. The way, the truth, and the life.

My prayer for each of us is that as we increase in maturity, sin will lose its allure. I'm praying that righteousness becomes the new glamorous.

Does your heart cry out,
"God, do You know I am a sinner?"
Then listen as our Lord speaks to you.
God replies to your struggling heart:

DO YOU KNOW WHO I AM? . . .
I AM your Savior.

You are not alone in your sin, because everyone on this earth has sinned and fallen short of My glory. I want you to know that I love you so much that I sent My one and only Son, Jesus, to be your Savior. To show you My love, while you were still a sinner, Jesus died for you to take away the penalty of your sin. He becomes your Savior if you believe in Him. I did not send Jesus to condemn you, but to save you from your sin.

Draw near to Me, confess your sins, and let Me forgive you of your sin and cleanse your guilty conscience. I AM able to keep you from falling from now on. I AM faithful and I will not let you be tempted beyond what you can bear. You can live a new life.

Sin does not have to be your master. Because I AM your Savior, you can live in grace, not in bondage to sin. I want you to live like you are dead to sin and alive to me!

Nothing can ever separate you from My love. I AM for you so that no one can be against you.

You are My beloved and I AM your Savior.
Forever and ever, amen.[1]

Where can I go from your Spirit?
Where can I flee from your presence?
If I go up to the heavens, you are there;
if I make my bed in the depths, you are there.
—PSALM 139:7–8

CHAPTER SEVEN

DO YOU KNOW
I AM LONELY?

He Is Here

I remember lonely.

I remember the kind of lonely that drains your soul and whispers sadness to your heart.

Tonight I am in another hotel room, my fifth in six days. The view is beautiful. The people have been gracious and kind. But I am just so very lonely now and I want to go home. Wonderful places aren't very wonderful if there is no one to turn to and say, "Look at that!"

Normally I am gone from home for only one night, but somehow lots of speaking engagements ran together and the travel was crazy, so I've been away from the people I love for about ten days in a row. I will never let this happen again. It's too hard. And the really great ministry that I am doing is woven with a thick cord of loneliness that makes each hour feel heavy. I remember this kind of loneliness. This week is just a small reminder, but I have lived this kind of desperate emptiness before.

There were the seven and a half years I lived as a single mom, the years when my babies were small (all four born in seven years), and the painful year I lived as a single woman on staff at a church in a city where I didn't know anyone. The ache I feel tonight is all too familiar to me.

Through the years I've made my own lonely list. Lonely is:

- No one worried whether my plane landed safely.
- Living in a house full of people, but feeling unknown.
- Room service for one.
- No one waiting for me in the "kiss and cry" at the airport.
- No last call just to say good night.
- An empty bed and plenty of room for all my clothes in the closet.
- Rolling the trash to the street at midnight because there is no one to say, "Oh, I'll get that."
- Having something fabulous to say but no one to listen.
- Having no one to hold me.

I bet that at some time in your life, you had a lonely list too. Maybe you have one today. Maybe your empty heart spills over to God and asks, "Do You know how very lonely I am?"

Someone has said that the word *loneliness* was created to express the pain of being alone. The word *solitude* was created to express the glory of being alone. We all know the difference. I love solitude. I crave it. My time of solitude fills me up and makes me a better wife, mom, and lover of God. I really only need about two hours, every so often. Loneliness, on the other hand, has made me feel like I would surely die from its pain.

Last night I went to sleep in this very nice room, snuggled into a very nice bed. And my tears leaked onto a very nice pillowcase. I lay there and thought to myself, "Angela, you are going home in a couple of days. This lonely ache will be relieved. Then you will get all the touch-touch, hug-hug love you can handle (my love language). Maybe tonight,

> *The word* loneliness *was created to express the pain of being alone. The word* solitude *was created to express the glory of being alone.*

you should pray for the truly lonely. I know you remember what it feels like."

The very first person I prayed for is my very dear girlfriend, a single mom of four who is so incredibly alone. Somehow she manages to provide exactly what that family needs, but they never have anything extra. She doesn't have any family close; her mom passed away fifteen years ago and there is no one for my girlfriend to lean on. I'm eight hours away from her and I know that many days and, especially, nights, she is desperately lonely and even afraid. Last night I prayed for her to be loved. *Oh Lord, would You send her love and comfort and peace?*

As I kept praying, I remembered a couple raising their special-needs son. His condition makes them feel lonely, like no one else understands how intense every single day is for them. *God, please hold them up. Give them hope beyond measure and come with an answer for the loneliness they bear.*

Another friend just lost his family in divorce, the kids won't call or write, and now this latest recession has taken his business and his home. The bankruptcy hearing is on Monday. The whole stinking mess seems unbearable. How can one person hold up under such heartache? *Oh God, I am praying into his loneliness. Please strengthen this man with Your courage and Your grace. Can You give him a glimpse of a brighter future?*

> A study by the American Council of Life Insurance reported that the most lonely group in America is college students. Next on the list are divorced people, welfare recipients, single mothers, rural students, housewives, and the elderly.[1]

Now, this morning, I am praying for you and for the lonely place inside of you. Proximity to people may have no bearing on whether or not you feel lonely. Women are lonely in their marriages and inside houses full of busy children. We might be lonely at church. We can be lonely in small towns and big cities. Tim Hansel has said, "Loneliness is not the same as being alone. Loneliness is feeling alone . . . no matter how many people are around you. It is a feeling of being disconnected, unplugged, left out, isolated."[2] Loneliness is a feeling, not necessarily a circumstance.

Our Savior Knew Our Loneliness

Even our Jesus led a life woven with threads of loneliness. As the perfect Son of God, He was certainly unlike all the other children who grew up around Him in Nazareth. Feeling different from everyone else creates feelings of loneliness, and Jesus, who was fully human, must have felt that during His childhood and into adulthood.

After Jesus began His ministry, there were occasions that the disciples, His closest friends, denied Him and abandoned Him. At the time of His greatest sorrow, the few who remained had scattered, leaving Him utterly alone. Jesus certainly knew the pain of our loneliness.

> For we do not have a high priest who is unable to sympathize
> with our weaknesses, but we have one who has been tempted in
> every way, just as we are—yet was without sin. Let us then approach the throne of grace with confidence, so that we may receive mercy and find grace to help us in our time of need.
>   —Hebrews 4:15-16

The Scriptures refer to Jesus as our sympathetic High Priest. Hebrews says that Jesus "shared in [our] humanity" (2:14), and that He was "like his brothers in every way" (2:17). He knew the same loneliness that you and I encounter this very day.

And so I believe this is where we are supposed to begin. With Jesus. People will disappoint us. A friend intends to be consistent but sometimes can't come through. Our families can't be with us in every circumstance. But Jesus is the One who never fails. He hears even the most faint whisper that we pray. He understands how loneliness can grip the heart and paralyze the soul. In our loneliness, let us turn to the only One who is able. Maybe you can say something like this:

Jesus, my heart is so lonely today and I ache from its emptiness. I know You must surely understand. Would You
come and give me comfort? Speak Your tenderness into
my soul. Please make these feelings subside so that there
is peace inside of me instead. I want Your peace, oh God. I
need Your mercy. I lay my loneliness on Your altar. There
is nowhere else for me to go. Please fill me with Your presence and give to me Your thoughts. I love You. I need You.
Amen.

All through history and the Scriptures, men and women have
faced great challenges that made them become fearful or lonely.
Their circumstances made them doubt their calling or feel anxious about their abilities. But an awareness of God's presence
became their strength. The lonely became courageous, bold, and
filled with hope.

> In my own case I just determined I would be satisfied with
> God alone. I gave up seeking after any feeling of satisfaction,
> and consented to go through all the rest of my life with no
> feeling whatever, if this should be God's will. I said, "Lord,
> you are enough for me, just yourself, without any of your
> gifts or your blessings. I have you, and I am content. I will be
> content, I choose to be content, I am content." I said this by
> faith. I still have to say it by faith often. I have to do so this
> very evening, for I am not very well, and feel, what I expect
> thou would call "low." But it makes no difference how I feel.
> He is just the same, and he is with me, and I am His, and I am
> satisfied.[3]
>
> —HANNAH WHITALL SMITH

That same awareness will give strength to you and me. God is
with you. He will never forget you. He sympathizes in your loneliness and gives a comfort to hold you through these days. Jesus not
only knows, He comes to minister to your heart.

Made for Companionship

I believe there are at least two sides to our loneliness. The first is our need for companionship. The second is our soul's longing for God. I love that in the very first book of the Bible, God spoke to our need for companionship. He declared to all of Creation, "It's not good for the Man to be alone; I'll make a him a helper, a companion" (Genesis 2:18, MESSAGE).

My daddy has always had such a huge sensitivity to my loneliness. When I was in seminary, he flew my mama to Texas one week because he thought I was getting too lonely. All my life he has said things like, "Too much alone is not good for you. . . . Loneliness makes your mind play tricks on you. . . . The house can get too quiet." I can't tell you how many times my parents have shown up at just the right time because something told my dad I had been alone long enough.

I'm praying to have the same sensitivity with my children. My college freshman texted to me last night, "Mama, I'm just so lonely." My heart broke thinking that right in the middle of thousands of students on a Christian campus, my baby is aching with loneliness. So I told her this morning, "We'll be there on Sunday." I could hear the relief in her voice. A little hope. They say that our brain produces electrical impulses called "joy" when you believe someone is happy to see you. We're gonna go and give Taylor some joy. The Lord spoke so powerfully to all of us, it's not good to be alone.

Last year when I was married, my deep, deep longing for companionship was satisfied like I have never experienced before. Before Scott, I had lived in a wonderful home with my four children. We had great neighbors and friends, a loving church family, and my parents close by. But the ache to be specially known by someone was ever-present. I longed to have someone to share the beautiful and the difficult. Someone to talk through parenting ideas with. Someone to dream the future with. God made each one of us long for intimacy and love, even though many of us have learned how to deny the longing. I believe that God intended that we would live this life among a variety of companions: our family, children, friends, co-workers, and the body of Christ. Each one giving a piece of companionship that soothes many aches of our loneliness. We are never alone. Jesus said in John 14:

> I will talk to the Father, and he'll provide you another Friend so that you will always have someone with you. This Friend is the Spirit of Truth. The godless world can't take him in because it doesn't have eyes to see him, doesn't know what to look for. But you know him already because he has been staying with you, and will even be *in* you!
>
> —JOHN 14:16–17 (MESSAGE)

I AM Your God Who Is Here

Maybe you realize that right where you are today, it's not good for you to be alone either. A lonely place inside of you reminds you that you were made for companionship. Here is the first thing I want you to know about the character of God: He is near to you right where you are, no matter how alone you may feel. God is omnipresent in His character, which means that He is essentially present in all places and present at all times. There is nowhere you can be where God is not, and there is nowhere you can go without Him. He is here. Jesus says to us, "Surely I am with you always, to the very end of the age" (Matthew 28:20).

Now read this beautiful truth about God: "God makes a home for the lonely" (Psalm 68:6, NASB). First you need to know that God sees your longing for companionship; He is with you always. And He makes a home for you. You and I belong to the family of God, the body of Christ. If you find yourself without loving companionship, I'd say to you today, turn toward the home God has made for you inside His family, made up of the followers of Christ.

There is absolutely no way I could have lived a healthy solo mom life for all those years without the companionship and encouragement of Christ's followers. Truly, I can't imagine how overwhelming life might have become for me. These were the people who cared for my heart, stopped by our home just to see if we needed anything, brought us meals, fixed our overflowing potty, and invited me to their family's Mother's Day lunch because my kids were with their dad that day.

A Few Truths About Loneliness

I also know that the sweet companionship of friends might not be all you long for. You may long to be loved, long for intimacy, long for one special person to call you his. You are waiting for your lonely heart to be loved. Here are a few truths I learned in my lonely waiting. I pass them along to you praying they become an encouragement.

Lonely Will Not Kill You

Though it feels like you just might die from the pain, I can testify that God gives a grace even when you believe you can't go on one more day. Remember this passage: "The LORD is close to the brokenhearted and saves those who are crushed in spirit" (Psalm 34:18). For the woman who belongs to God, the crushing weight of loneliness cannot steal your life or your future. I promise that God is still on the throne of heaven. Nothing comes to either of us without passing through this sovereign hand. And the promises of God still hold.

Even though loneliness can make you feel like your life will never be whole again, God says He "is able to do immeasurably more than all we ask or imagine, according to his power that is at work within us" (Ephesians 3:20).

I know you might ache with pain in your longing for companionship. Some days I cried and cried over my own loneliness. But I know God still has a great, big life for each one of us, waiting to be lived with passion and purpose. I do not think we are called to live as lonely people. God is here. He knows all your longings.

Lonely Must Be Lived with Integrity

Let me just say this: loneliness does not mean we are desperate. We are not desperate people who have to make irrational choices based on our emptiness. Maybe you need to say to yourself, "I am not desperate." We belong to God for goodness' sake. And the woman of God is called to walk through her loneliness with integrity.

I've watched too many people make choices out of their lonely hearts. They end up talking to people they have no business talking to, meeting people in chat rooms they have no business chatting with, dating the wrong guys over and over again, marrying, divorcing, and doing the whole crazy cycle over again. In case you missed it, we all have stupid potential and many of us can be stupid twice.

God calls us to live with integrity, even when it hurts. I've said to women all over this country, "Take a Tylenol PM and go to bed!" I get it. I remember so vividly how the nighttime exaggerated my pain. My bed felt so big. The house was too quiet. Every creak and noise seemed louder and scarier. I completely understand why women make dumb choices from that kind of pain, but we just cannot do that. God is calling us to wait through our loneliness with a greater degree of integrity.

Early in my single mom years, I realized that Satan whispered to me at night. After I had tucked all the kids into bed, while my bedside light was still on, he reminded me how alone I was and taunted me with that truth. If I were ever going to break down and cry, it would be at night, mostly between nine and eleven. It turns out that's about the time most people do the dumbest things. I realized those people are choosing from their emptiness and their loneliness. I was lonely and I was not exempt from being dumb too. So I began to take a Tylenol PM in the evenings at about 8:30. After I tucked the kids into bed, I was ready to read a few pages and fall fast asleep. For me, it seemed like the smartest thing to cut the loneliest hours out of my day. I was always strong in the mornings, but the night was when lonely screamed for me.

In my youth group days I taught my kids to say, "Integrity is what you do when no one is looking." It matters how we face our lonely circumstances, and I believe with all my heart that we can do that for the glory of God.

Be very careful, then, how you live—not as unwise but as wise,
making the most of every opportunity, because the days are evil.
Therefore do not be foolish, but understand what the Lord's will is.
—EPHESIANS 5:15–17

When I met my husband, Scott, he had lived the six years before
I met him and since the end of his marriage remaining physically
pure and living with integrity. Instead of a Tylenol PM, he trained
his body for triathlons, alternating his running, biking, and swim-
ming for the mornings and nights around his work. I cried when he
told me that in those years, he had decided he would probably die a
lonely old man. I will never forget his answer when I asked, "What
kept you pure all these years?"

His tender reply will tell you a lot about his heart. Scott said, "I
just always believed that somewhere, somehow, God would bless
my life if I lived right."

And God does bless the righteous. He honors the woman who
faces her loneliness and then decides to live with integrity. It's
God's character to add blessing to right living and, conversely, to
allow consequences for disobedience.

Let's live underneath the promised blessing that comes to right
choices even in lonely circumstances.

Loneliness Can Teach You How to Love

If we will let it, loneliness will teach us how to live grateful lives
and to love the ones God has given us to love. In my darkest single
mom days, desperately alone while the children were with their dad, God gave me a deep gratefulness for simple things. I learned that even in

> God will honor the woman who faces her loneliness and then de-cides to live with integrity.

my ache, I could tell God thank You for the warm cup of coffee in
the morning. The call from my neighbor just to check on me came
to mean so much in my loneliness. I was so very thankful for the
concern. My grateful quotient began to grow in that dark place
of lonely. And then, I think I learned to love with greater passion

because the loneliness had taught me to be grateful for love. There are lessons in the loneliness if we will look for them.

Longing for God

There has always been an ache inside of me. I remember it as a little girl, a college student, in marriage, and in my single mom life. As I entered my forties, the tiny ache began to whisper a pondering type of question, "Is this all there is? So this is living. This is having a family. This is it. Hmmm."

I think the loneliness some of us experience, even when our lives are full, is the heart longing to be home with the Lord.

Nothing earth-shattering or crazy-making, just an ache for something more. And the ache always seems to give a sense of loneliness. I have come to recognize that little tenderness inside of me as a longing for God.

I believe the soul was made for a perfect, intimate relationship with our Creator. But we live in a fallen world, only knowing in part, seeing in a mirror dimly. We have a relationship with our God, but not the one we will one day know in heaven. I think the loneliness some of us experience, even when our lives are full, is the heart longing to be home with the Lord.

There is a reason we can be in a room full of people we love and still suffer a twinge of loneliness. Most of us are not completely removed from people and we have a variety of people we love in our lives. I am sure you have known this same longing in your busy life. You may be married, live in a dorm full of people, work alongside many co-workers, or attend a church full of believers. Or maybe you have little children playing at your feet right this minute, and yet, truth be told, your soul can whisper that it longs for more.

I believe the second side of loneliness is a hole in our heart that longs to be filled. But it cannot be completely filled by another human being or things on this earth. That empty place inside of us was made for more. It was made for God. Sometimes we can get the emptiness turned upside-down and begin to think the *more* we need is more stuff or more people or more accomplishment. But the soul longs for more of God. Do not confuse your need for Him with an attraction to things.

Truth is, I don't really need another thing on this earth. Actually, I do need some food every day, but not as much as I have. And if I could fit into all the clothes in my closet, I'm sure I would have enough to wear for a lifetime or two. We have a home with enough beds and furniture to house our clan. A backyard to romp around in and cars to drive. We have plenty of stuff, and thankfully I learned a long time ago that new stuff is only a temporary delight. Maybe about fifteen minutes of fun. A gift from our Father to be enjoyed, but more stuff fills nothing in the soul.

Nowadays, when I feel that little pang of loneliness, most of the time I recognize it for what it is. "Oh, this is my heart longing for home. To know God perfectly. To experience His perfect intimacy. To celebrate His perfect presence. To live every moment in the place I was made to be." But until then, until heaven, you and I have been assigned to this earth. This beautiful, fallen, crazy, wonderful place to live. And the question becomes, "How do we live with the pang of lonely until we see God?"

Acknowledge That This Isn't Home

Just finally understanding what is going on in my heart has changed so much about how I navigate these twinges of loneliness. I'm learning to allow those pangs to remind me of my home in heaven. I will even say to myself, "I'm longing for home right now," and almost every time that truth stills my heart. I remember that I am made for a perfect relationship that I do not yet have with my Father, and there is a still and quiet hope in that.

> Why are you downcast, O my soul?
> Why so disturbed within me?
> Put your hope in God,
> for I will yet praise him,
> my Savior and my God.

—PSALM 43:5

Accept No Cheap Imitations

Our human response to emptiness is to try to find anything to feel full again. One little hunger pain and I'm in the kitchen looking for a cracker. But we must pay attention to this longing for God. What we know is that it cannot be filled with anything or any person on this earth. God is the only One who soothes that longing. And so, in our spiritual maturity, we have to learn to take that longing to God. Don't be fooled into thinking that a new shirt or a new house or a new man will fill that place that was made for God. Every single thing you try to throw toward that longing will be temporary and shallow. It's like eating cotton candy when you're starving; there is some momentary satisfaction, but the hunger remains and grows. Do not allow yourself to be tricked by the schemer, Satan. He would love to trip you up for years, taking you down dead-end roads when in truth your heart is trying to get to God.

Worship Him

The most right and soul-filling response to a longing for God is to worship Him. Maybe you have experienced something like this . . . your week has been full and crazy busy, the weekend filled with soccer games and birthday parties. Sunday morning you get everyone up, dressed, fed, and out the door to church. You drop one at the nursery, check a couple others into their classes, and finally plop into a seat, taking a couple of minutes to say hi to a friend or look at your bulletin. But then the worship begins, and you remember God is here. The soothing power of worship spills over you, filling your heart like nothing else could.

But worship isn't just for Sunday morning and you don't have to be led by anyone else to get there. Worship is the heart crying out to God, "You are here. You are mighty. You are able. You are glorious. There is none like You. Thank You for saving me. Thank You for loving me. Thank You for promising I'll be with You forever." Our hearts can worship in a multitude of places, in a million different ways. The point is to worship God. With our lives, in our families, in our work . . . as we go . . . we can worship God.

Find Your Purpose

I believe one of the greatest gifts I have been given is that every single day when I wake up, I am absolutely certain what I was put on this earth for. I am the mother of four, the wife of one, and called to teach the Bible with every creative fiber inside of me. One of the worst decisions I ever made was about twenty years ago when I studied for a real estate license. I have no idea what I was think-ing. I had a master's degree from seminary. I knew very clearly that God had called me to ministry, so what in the world was I doing in real estate classes? I had lost sight of my purpose. Needless to say, my real estate career was a bust and those years were very lonely times. A huge part of the loneli-ness was that I had turned away from my God purpose.

> A million other people have great ideas about what you and I should be doing. But we must stay with God's calling for our lives.

Many days I say to myself, "Be the mama, be the wife, be the teacher. Period." I have to tell myself to stay with God's purpose for me. A million other people have great ideas about what you and I should be doing. But we must stay with God's calling for our lives.

Live with Passion

I don't run into many people who are having a good time, but when I do, wow, do those people light up the room. I believe the woman who follows Christ is called to live a passionate life. We are sup-posed love big and care deeply. We are supposed to bear His wit-ness in our spirit.

My dad checked into the hospital last week for what turned out to be too much cold medicine making his heart beat fast. He told me that the nurse who checked him in said, "You know Jesus, don't you?"

He replied to her, "As a matter of fact, I do. How did you know?"

This complete stranger said, "I could see it in your spirit." My daddy is a passionate man who is happy to be alive. Passion trumps loneliness every day of the week. Living with God in view, thankful for the life He has given to us, and giving to others a graciousness and joy is a beautiful reflection of God's filling our longing.

Trust in His Everlasting Love

One of the most beautiful character traits of God is that His love for us is everlasting (Jeremiah 31:3). That means nothing you can ever do will subtract from His love or bring His love to an end. Like wayward children of a loving parent, we can grieve the heart of God with our choices, but His love endures, covering our sins with His forgiveness and grace.

In the darkest times, when our spirits are lonely and our souls downcast, you and I must lean into the everlasting love that God promises to us. Psalm 136 says twenty-six times that God's steadfast love endures forever. I think the writer wanted to make sure that we get it. God's love never fails. He never steps away or turns His back. We are loved. Purely, freely, and lavishly loved by the Almighty God. His plans for us are more than we could ever dream for ourselves. Let the truth of God's love make you curious. *I wonder what God is up to? Where will this journey take me?* And then put your weight down on His love.

Keep Eternity in View

Maybe every loneliness and every struggle finds its proper significance in light of this one thing—we are on our way home. Hallelujah. For the woman who belongs to Christ, these burdens may be wearying and many days may be lonesome, but not one heartache will have the final say. Jesus has gone ahead to prepare a place for us so that we can walk through this world with eternity in view.

Does your heart cry out,
"God, do You know I am lonely?"
Then listen as our Lord speaks to you.
God replies to your lonely heart:

DO YOU KNOW WHO I AM? . . .
I AM here.

There is no place you can go from My presence. If you go to the
heavens I AM there. If you go underground, I AM there. I see how

loneliness makes you feel like no one cares for you. I see your tender heart. I hear your quiet cries.

I want you to understand that I am not far off and watching from a distance; I AM here, in the very room where you sit, I AM right here with you. This place on earth is your temporary home, but one day you will be where your heart longs to go. You will be with Me forever.

Turn your focus toward Me so that My presence can give you comfort. I AM your God of compassion. I AM the one who will trade your despair for a garment of praise; I AM the God who can renew your spirit, restore your joy, and hold you up by the power of My Spirit.

Trust that I AM here for you. I AM your refuge to run to. I AM the fortress that keeps you safe. Because of My great love, this loneliness will not consume you. My compassion will not fail you. Every morning you will see the new mercy of My faithfulness to you.

Put your hope in Me. Seek after Me. Wait for Me.

> *You are My beloved and I AM here.*
> *Forever and ever, amen.*[4]

[God] gives power to the weak,
and to those who have no might He increases strength.
—ISAIAH 40:29 (NKJV)

CHAPTER EIGHT

DO YOU KNOW
I AM UNDISCIPLINED?

He Is My Strength

I just got married.

About ten months ago, I was married to Scott, the most beautiful man I have ever met. I wanted to look really cute for him on our wedding day. And when you are forty-five and have given birth to four babies, giving yourself to a man is, oh my goodness, a very scary thought.

So, five months before the wedding, I began going to Jenny Craig. I did everything she said and never cheated, and in a matter of months had lost about twenty pounds. I was also going to see my trainer, Clayton, and working out two or three times a week. Thinking about that honeymoon kept me motivated and serious about the task ahead. People would offer me "just a bite," and I always turned them down. I've never been more committed to something than I was about trying to get skinny before the wedding.

All in all, things were going along pretty well, except that when my dress came in, three days before the wedding, we almost couldn't get it zipped in the back. I wish I were kidding. I had no idea that you have to order a wedding dress at least four months in advance, so I didn't give myself enough time. I truly thought I could just stop into a little shop and pick one up. So it had to be rushed and then it only arrived because the store owner called several times each day pestering the manufacturer and finally getting that thing overnighted to us.

According to my measurements and the dressmaker's guide to measurements in the huge wedding dress binder, the dress should have fit. But it didn't. With a girdle and two people working the back, we could get the dress zipped, but then we all held our breath in unison, waiting for an explosion, anywhere, any second. Standing in the bridal store, I stood looking at this unbelievable mistake shrink-wrapped around my body and tried not to lose it. All the wedding boutique ladies said with halfhearted encouragement, "It doesn't look like it's too tight." So I tried to rein in my disappointment and get some perspective. It was just a dress for one night. If I stood still it did look okay, and maybe I could bunny-hop down the aisle since I couldn't actually take a step in the thing.

The miracle-worker alterations lady thought she could let one seam out about half an inch. I told her I'd take it. When we picked up the dress two days later I could barely tell a difference, but I had no options. That was the dress I was wearing for my very special wedding to my very special man. I figured I would have to eat standing up at the reception because sitting would have been certain disaster.

That night, my friend Lisa threw me in the car about 8 P.M. We had one hour before the stores closed and she was on a mission: to find a dress I could eat dinner in. Amazingly, the only store we could think of was still open. They had some prom dresses left and we found the most flowing, short, black, perfect-for-dinner dress you could imagine, on sale! My wedding reception was saved from the embarrassment of a wardrobe malfunction, and I got to pretend I was Hannah Montana, changing outfits between sets.

I can't even imagine what would have happened if I hadn't carried on with Jenny Craig while that dress was being made. I had worked hard, stayed the course, and even with the tight dress, it felt good to do my very best in the months before the wedding.

Now you have to know, I married a great man and one of the things we enjoy together is travel and food. We began our marriage with a honeymoon in Florence, Italy, with some of the most wonderful food in the world. The problem is that I haven't stopped eating since the honeymoon. Well, I have stopped eating like a crazy woman now, but now is twenty-five pounds later. Yep, I have gained back all my Jenny Craig weight plus five. What a bummer.

Scott is an iron man competitor, so he can eat almost whatever he wants. I am not a competitor, which is another story, but basically it means I should not eat whatever I want.

My friend Carlye is the great encourager. She is the one who sent me to Jenny Craig before my wedding. She cheered as each pound melted away. And just a few days ago she was so sweet on the phone. I was whining about not having anything to wear because my clothes

> *Yep, I have gained back all my Jenny Craig weight plus five. What a bummer.*

don't fit and Carlye said, "Aw, honey, you're happy. People eat when they're happy." She's right. I am very happy, and these are the happiest pounds I've ever known, but good grief, I have to stop eating.

The bigger question about my eating is, why is self-discipline so hard?

Last weekend, I was sitting beside my friend Julie, and yet again fussing about my tight clothes. "If I could find the switch for self-discipline, we could rescue the world."

Nodding in agreement, she whispered back, "Call me when you have it."

The struggle here is not just about twenty-five pounds. Mine is the ongoing battle to find self-discipline in many areas of my life. Of course, I have met people who are so disciplined that they have no life, and that is not what I long for. I want enough discipline to live at my God-given potential. The best version of who I can be, given my circumstances, my physical body, and my mind. I just want the Lord to reach down and turn on the switch of self-control inside my head. It seems like it must have a short flickering on and off inside of me. Little power surges for a season. Blackouts in others.

Maybe you feel the same way.

There is a legend at Harvard that the late Le Baron Russel Briggs, beloved dean of the College, once asked a student why he had failed to complete an assignment.

"I wasn't feeling very well, sir," said the student. "Mr. Smith," said the Dean, "I think that in time you may perhaps find that most of the work of the world is done by people who aren't feeling very well."[1]

—Frederick Lewis Allen

Why can't I just say to myself, *Get up early tomorrow morning to take a walk,* and then just pop right up and do that? Why can't I let the kids eat cheesecake without taking a bite, or two? Why can't I just sit down and turn out a book like so-and-so? (I'm sure God knows who I'm talking about.) Goodness, I could begin making a list of "*Why can't I's,*" but that is not the point of this chapter. The idea is to find God. To take the honesty of my great need to Him and let the truths of Scripture settle into my soul. I desire to know God's response to this longing. *Oh Lord, do You know that I am undisciplined?*

Father, I want this so badly. I long for more self-discipline, for self-control. Do You know that I long for more personal discipline in all the areas of my life? In my spiritual life with You, I want to actually give to You as my heart desires to give. With full consistency. Full passion. Full worship. More discipline and focus. The next level above here.

In my physical body, if only there were more discipline that leads to greater energy, greater health, and even the ability to give more to the ones I love. Oh Lord, do You know how much I long for increased discipline with my body?

With my mind, staying with an organized plan, or keeping a routine that I've started, or even maintaining the bins Lisa made to keep everything sorted in my office. Oh God, do You know that greater discipline for my mind could affect so many things?

Why is this so hard? Lord, please show me Your heart in this. I know You can't possibly expect perfection from me, so what is Your desire? Will this longing be answered inside of me on this earth? Does a person have to come wired a certain way from birth, or can this struggle be overcome in anyone?

Oh, God, please hear my honest heart. I want to know Your will for me. I want Your power and Your strength. I long to be the woman I dream of being and I am so tired of doing the same things when I desperately want to do better. Please speak to me in ways I can understand and apply to my life. Would You be clear with me? Make me less and less like the woman I have been, more and more like the woman You see I can be.

Amen and amen.

I am not lazy, at least about most things, but what is it about some things that seems to chain me to my lack of control? How can a person be so diligent and yet not? The struggle is intense. I long for greater self-discipline. I want to live in victory, in the big things and the small.

The Struggle Within

As I began studying for this chapter and wrestling with my own longing to know greater self-discipline, my mind immediately returned to the vulnerable words of the apostle Paul. Somehow, I took comfort in his honesty. He so perfectly explains my heart, and probably yours as well.

> I do not understand what I do. For what I want to do I do not do, but what I hate I do. . . . For I have the desire to do what is good, but I cannot carry it out. For what I do is not the good I want to do; no, the evil I do not want to do—this I keep on doing. . . .
> So I find this law at work: When I want to do good, evil is right there with me. For in my inner being I delight in God's law; but I see another law at work in the members of my body, waging war against the law of my mind and making me a prisoner of the law of sin at work within my members.
> —Romans 7:15, 18–19, 21–23

Paul says that he knows what he longs to do and how he longs to live, but inside of him there is a war waging, good against evil. The flesh against the Spirit. That same war goes on inside each one of us too. There is the good that we want to do to improve ourselves and the pull of our flesh, the old nature, that pulls at us to distract us from what is right.

> For the sinful nature desires what is contrary to the Spirit, and
> the Spirit what is contrary to the sinful nature. They are in con-
> flict with each other, so that you do not do what you want.
> —GALATIANS 5:17

The struggle that you and I wrestle with every day is a very real spiritual battle going on inside the mind. You can feel it, I know you can. You know how very real and strong this battle inside each one of us is.

My current struggles involve diet and exercise. Maybe your current struggles are very different. Maybe you keep finding yourself involved with the wrong people, maybe even in abusive relationships, and you ask, *Why do I keep making the same choices when in my mind I know better?* Maybe you wrestle with an addiction to food, gambling, drugs, or maybe undisciplined spending is your battle. In your heart you truly desire freedom and a life free of addiction, but the war inside of you keeps you in chains. Maybe you want to spend time with God every single day, but more often than not, something distracts you from the very thing you want to do.

No matter how you define your struggle, the longing for greater self-discipline is a very real spiritual battle that each one of us must acknowledge as present and powerful inside of us.

As we read Paul's words of struggle, we can also take heart. Paul goes on to give us the only hope we have for greater discipline and self-control:

> Who will rescue me from this body of death? Thanks be to
> God—through Jesus Christ our Lord!
> —ROMANS 7:24–25

Paul says that our only rescue from the war in our flesh comes from God through Jesus Christ. He goes on to say that we can be controlled by the sinful nature that is still inside of us or we can live according to the guidance of the Spirit and focus our minds on what the Spirit desires for us.

> Those who live according to the sinful nature have their minds set on what that nature desires; but those who live in accordance with the Spirit have their minds set on what the Spirit desires. The mind of sinful man is death, but the mind controlled by the Spirit is life and peace.
>
> —ROMANS 8:5–6

God's answer for this very real need is that we choose to live according to the will and the way of the Holy Spirit who has come to live inside of every believer. The Spirit is our help. He is our prayer partner and intercessor. He gives strength and step-by-step instructions. We must learn to listen and follow His voice inside of us.

> In the same way, the Spirit helps us in our weakness. We do not know what we ought to pray for, but the Spirit himself intercedes for us with groans that words cannot express. And he who searches our hearts knows the mind of the Spirit, because the Spirit intercedes for the saints in accordance with God's will.
>
> —ROMANS 8:26–27

Living On Fire

Truly, the longer God allows me to live on this earth, the more I desire to please Him. To imitate Him. To become the woman He sees in me. When my son William is on the soccer field and we see him connect all his skill and energy to play like a crazy man, we yell to him, "You're on firrrah!" Every capacity of his body and mind is engaged. And the coolest thing is that when he's playing like that, he's having the time of his life.

I want to live like that. Having the time of my life. Fully engaged. Learning to listen to the promptings of the Holy Spirit and then, the biggie, obeying God with all of my heart.

> Do you not know that in a race all the runners run, but only one
> gets the prize? Run in such a way as to get the prize. Everyone
> who competes in the games goes into strict training. They do it to
> get a crown that will not last; but we do it to get a crown that will
> last forever. Therefore I do not run like a man running aimlessly;
> I do not fight like a man beating the air. No, I beat my body and
> make it my slave so that after I have preached to others, I myself
> will not be disqualified for the prize.
>
> —1 CORINTHIANS 9:24–27

Paul, the same man who struggled with the battle of his flesh versus God's Spirit in the Romans passage, now writes that living the life God has called us to live requires training. A process. Becoming self-disciplined and controlled takes commitment, sacrifice, and focus.

I love that as I am writing to you, God is reminding me of Scripture truths I learned long ago. It's amazing how as life goes by even a Christian can lose sight of powerful truths that transform our lives. Peter wrote to the followers of Christ,

> Therefore, I will always be ready to remind you of these things,
> even though you already know them, and have been established
> in the truth which is present with you. I consider it right, as long
> as I am in this earthly dwelling, to stir you up by way of reminder.
>
> —2 PETER 1:12–13 (NASB)

Maybe you are like me and the idea of training yourself to become self-disciplined is not new, but the fresh reminders from Scripture are beginning to relight the fires of desire anew inside you.

This morning I have a free day between speaking in one town and flying to another. Instead of spending the day traveling home and then right back out again, my husband thought I should stay put and write. God bless him. And so, right here in my hotel room, there is a new beginning for me. One can't write a chapter about self-discipline without being convicted right to the core. I am convicted. I desire the discipline God can give.

I was up late last night studying the passages we've been talking about, and the fresh desire to live them is burning inside of me. So I've set a couple of small goals for myself. Today I am planning to take two thirty-minute walks, one this morning and one around sunset. And I'm also committing to drinking four bottles of water because I never drink enough water. I imagine that may sound pretty easy to you, but for me, it's a serious beginning.

You see, I always sacrifice exercise when I have a deadline or lots to do. I know I shouldn't, but I feel guilty for taking the time away. No one else makes me feel guilty, it's just me, talking myself into a tizzy over how much there is to do. I am completely aware that I have it all turned upside-down. I should exercise, make my body stronger, and then there would be more of me to give to my work and family. I feel like Paul saying, "I know the good thing I am supposed to do and I still do the other."

So today, with these new reminders and this fresh desire, I am beginning. As I type these words, I am also praying for you, that God would be stirring up a renewed desire to live a disciplined life. In this next section, I want to lay out the order God has given to us and, hopefully, even more encouragement for us to begin.

I AM Your God Who Gives Strength

It is as if God whispers, "I AM your strength. I AM the only way to live a disciplined life. I can rescue you from your struggles. You are unable on your own, but I am able to make all grace abound to you."

God knows how much we struggle. Goodness gracious, He knows and cares so deeply about the spiritual wrestling that goes on in our souls. Remember that Paul cried out in Romans 7, "Who will rescue me from this?" (v. 24). And immediately, God told him the answer in his spirit, "Thanks be to God—through Jesus Christ our Lord!"

Today, I want you to know that God sent His Son, Jesus, to be our rescuer! And through the power of the indwelling Holy Spirit, you and I can receive the power to live disciplined lives. The same answer that Paul received is our answer. Jesus is the One who will save us from our lack. Jesus promised for us the person and the work of the Holy Spirit, and the Spirit inside of us is powerful enough to overcome every lazy streak, every procrastination, and every distraction.

I believe that with all of my heart. It's just that we so easily lose focus. We forget that victory over these struggles comes from an intimate, consistent dependence on the Spirit of God inside of us.

Galatians 5 says, "But the fruit of the Spirit is . . . *self-control*. . . . Those who belong to Christ Jesus have crucified the sinful nature with its passions and desires. Since we live by the Spirit, let us keep in step with the Spirit" (Galatians 5:22–26). The Spirit of God, unleashed within us, bears fruit in our lives. And one of those fruits is the gift of self-control. You and I, no matter what kind of past choices we have made, can know that powerful working of self-control because the Spirit of God lives in us.

The definition of *self-discipline* is the ability to regulate one's conduct by principle and sound judgment, rather than by impulse, desire, or social custom.

Sounds easy enough, right? But here is the action required for each of us. We must *choose* to obey the Spirit. A lot of people choose the temptations of their flesh because they enjoy the "high" they get from their indulgence. They are free to choose anything, but keep choosing the bondage and hoping for some kind of a high. Most everybody knows it's a total dead end that leads to death instead of blessing, but amazingly many take that path anyway.

Here is one of the things God is showing me. When I have a choice in front of me, let's say I have the freedom to be lazy or the freedom to be self-disciplined and obey God, there is such a high that comes to me when I obey! And I love that high! I love knowing that even in secret, where no one could see, I had the option to go with my fleshly desire or obey the Spirit and I chose obedience.

Sometimes, when I am feeling sad or grumpy, over-loaded or lost, the only thing that makes me feel better is obeying the Spirit of God. If God is saying write, it just

> *When I have a choice in front of me, there is such a high that comes to me when I obey! And I love that high!*

won't do for me to fold the laundry. I need to get to writing. By the same token, if He is saying drop everything and spend the after-noon with my child, it will be torture for me to keep working when God has clearly told me otherwise.

Learning to obey the Spirit means that you are staying con-nected to the Spirit. The more you bathe your life in prayer, the more intimately you will hear the Spirit lead you. Down deep inside, you will hear from the Spirit, *Go, girl,* or *Turn away.* The perfect Spirit is able to lead us into God's perfect will for our lives. He is the One who can make us able. I believe that there is no power in the life of a woman who does not pray. God gives us the power to lead self-controlled lives because we ask and receive through this intimate relationship called prayer.

For the woman who is a Christ-follower, the kind of woman who wants to live "on firrrah," with her passion blazing, every day has to begin with a fresh commitment to be led by the Spirit of God. There is no better way to begin fresh than in prayer. This morning, I slipped out of my hotel bed, put towels on the floor, and then lay down across them. I chose to put my body and my mind in the presence of God, beginning the day in prayer, renewing my commitment to listen and follow His wisdom. And then I said to the Lord, "I want to be speedy. *Please make me quick to obey.*" Maybe it's just my personality, or maybe I see the days going by too fast, but I don't want to waste any time not obeying the direc-tion of the Spirit.

Recognition of our inability to live up to our deepest spiritual longings leads us to cast ourselves upon God's Spirit for power and victory. Failure to continue in reliance upon the power of the Spirit places us once again in a position inviting defeat.

Sanctification is a gradual process that repeatedly takes the believer through this recurring sequence of failure, through dependency upon self, to triumph through the indwelling Spirit.[2]

Where to Begin

After a daily commitment to live according to the Spirit, here comes the hinge, the place where this whole thing turns: you and I will have to physically and mentally *respond as He leads*. I think the Bible calls it obedience.

In his book *The Pillars of Christian Character,* John MacArthur suggests some ways to begin[3]:

Start with Small Things
Clean your room. Clean out your pantry. Clean out the backseat in your car. Probably, right this minute, the Spirit is whispering exactly which small step you can take to begin. Self-discipline cultivated in the seemingly mundane things of life will spill over into the spiritual realm.

Get Yourself Organized
Your closet. The top of your desk. Inside your drawers. Your calendar. Maybe it's time to run your life instead of your life running you.

Don't Constantly Seek to Be Entertained
What a powerful idea to teach our children and to reteach ourselves. Ever try to spend thirty minutes doing absolutely nothing? I've done it. And my squirming reminds me that I am too entertained, by work or by play; either one can fill all my time.

Be on Time
Be careful how you walk, not as unwise men, but as wise, making the most of your time, because the days are evil.

—Ephesians 5:15–16 (nasb).

Keep Your Word

Simply let your "Yes" be "Yes," and your "No," "No"; anything beyond this comes from the evil one.

—Matthew 5:37

Do the Most Difficult Tasks First

It's the same old idea from middle school. Do the hardest thing first and get it over with. "There are always too many people who reach for the stool when there is a piano to be moved."[4]

Finish What You Start

Maybe the idea is that we start only what God has called us to start.

Accept Correction

Listen to counsel and accept discipline, that you may be wise the rest of your days.

—Proverbs 19:20 (NASB)

He whose ear listens to the life-giving reproof will dwell among the wise. He who neglects discipline despises himself, but he who listens to reproof acquires understanding.

—Proverbs 15:31–32 (NASB)

Practice Self-Denial

Maybe you are like me and you need to start small in this—one hot Krispy Kreme doughnut instead of two. Setting the alarm clock to wake up ten minutes earlier. One quick walk around the block instead of heading for the sofa and HGTV. Tom Landry said, "The job of a football coach is to make men do what they don't want to do, in order to achieve what they've always wanted to be."

Welcome Responsibility

There comes a day for all of us when we step across the line and become grown-ups. I'm watching my nineteen-year-old daughter approach the line. The mature woman welcomes the responsibility to live an amazing life, the responsibility to love God well. Welcome what is in front of you and run toward it with a renewed desire to live victoriously.

A Word to the Lazy

You know, the Bible has a lot to say about sluggards, lazy people, and fools. I am pretty sure that I am not any one of those people, and yet, we all have to be on guard that none of their traits is ever allowed to take a place in our lives. If we continually allow ourselves to follow every desire and whim, before long the fruit of an undisciplined and self-centered life will begin to show. Solomon says many convicting things about such a life in the book of Proverbs:

> A little sleep, a little slumber,
> a little folding of the hands to rest—
> and poverty will come on you like a bandit
> and scarcity like an armed man.
>
> —PROVERBS 6:10–11

> Like a city whose walls are broken down is a man who lacks self-control.
>
> —PROVERBS 25:28

> As a door turns on its hinges, so a sluggard turns on his bed.
>
> —PROVERBS 26:14

> The sluggard buries his hand in the dish; he is too lazy to bring it back to his mouth.
>
> —PROVERBS 26:15

Maybe as you read through those passages, you could say to yourself, "I am not a sluggard." Most of us aren't, even though I do know a few. But probably there are areas in each of our lives where we have some slug potential. And it's the slug potential that we have to be aware of.

My slug potential just rewarded me with twenty-five extra pounds. By allowing myself to indulge my slug-ness, I have also allowed consequences into my life. I cannot wear one cute thing that is hanging in my closet, and inside of me, that really feels like sin. The extra weight makes me feel self-conscious, and that's exactly what I don't want to happen when my whole focus is supposed to be on God, teaching His Word, and loving the others He brings into my life. Because I made poor choices these past months, I just don't feel good. I'm not strong. My energy level is not where I like it. Discouragement and fatigue have been attached to the consequences.

No wonder Solomon had so much to say about the sluggard. It is totally the loser path in life. To avoid any slug potential, the woman of God is called to lead a self-disciplined life.

I believe God sees my heart in this. He hears me echo the words of Paul, "I know better and I want to do better. Oh Lord, by the power of the Holy Spirit, please make it so." And I believe God will be our strength. Strength to conquer each area of undiscipline. Strength for our spirit when discouragement sets in. Over and over, He renews our strength to face the next mountain with a godly discipline we could not find on our own.

Finally, be strong in the Lord and in the strength of His might.

—EPHESIANS 6:10 (NASB)

Allow me to give you an update on my weight-loss journey: Writing this chapter has been such a convicting journey for me. I am freshly reminded that I long to live in obedience. And obedience in the hard things is where I desperately need the gentle but firm reminders from my Father. He is the One who gives power.

Twelve pounds are gone, slowly, but hopefully for good. And I finally made appointments with a new trainer here in North Carolina. She has her work cut out for her, but I am lacing up my sneakers and going to see her, and that is obedience for me. May you be encouraged today. And may your journey toward discipline bring great glory to our God.

Does your heart cry out,
"God, do You know I am undisciplined?"
Then listen as our Lord speaks to you.
God replies to your struggling heart:

DO YOU KNOW WHO I AM? . . .
I AM your strength.

I AM robed in majesty and I wear the belt of strength. I AM where your help comes from. I want you to be wise and full of strength, wearing strength as your clothing. My Spirit is where your strength comes from, not your own might or power. I AM the one who arms you with strength.

Don't you know? I will renew your strength. I energize those who are tired and give fresh strength to the drop-outs. Sometimes My strength comes to you in quietness and confidence. Sometimes My strength comes while you wait for Me. Sometimes My joy will be your strength. Sometimes it is wisdom that brings you strength.

I have given you an entire armor to wear to give you strength in every way. You can do all things through Me. I will give you the strength.

You are my beloved and I AM your strength.
Forever and ever, amen.[5]

He who did not spare his own Son,
but gave him up for us all—
how will he not also, along with him,
graciously give us all things?
—ROMANS 8:32

CHAPTER NINE

DO YOU KNOW
I AM HESITANT?

He is Generous

I am the daughter of a produce man.

Back in Mount Airy, North Carolina, my dad, Joe, and his brother, Donald, went into business together. They cleaned up a building, bought a truck, and opened the doors of their business called Little Man Fruit Market. My dad and my uncle worked night and day, hauling produce from various markets and farms. I must have been about eight years old when they started, but I vividly remember afternoons sweeping the floors in this place that would become our "fruitstand." There was a wood-burning pot-bellied stove, more apples than one kid could ever eat, and it seems like it was always cold. I needed to stand close to the stove.

At some point the Thomas brothers had the opportunity to buy another fruit stand in Greensboro, North Carolina, and it was decided that my dad would move our family to the new town to run the business. I remember moving in the middle of fourth grade from Mrs. Ramey's class in Mount Airy into Mrs. Bradham's class in Greensboro. Both schools had orange Creamsicles, and even though I had to leave Jackie, I met Beth and Cindy and Renee, so it worked out.

Thomas Fruit Stand was a very busy place located on Highway 220 South, which just happened to be the road most folks took to Myrtle Beach. At first the fruit stand was popular because it was a bit of a tourist stop with people stocking up for their weekend getaway. Eventually, because my dad and my uncle were men of such great integrity, people drove from all over, year-round, to buy the freshest produce anyone could find.

My dad worked about twenty hours a day, getting up every morning at 1 or 2 A.M. to haul produce in for the fruit stand, and it was usually after nine each night when he came home. After about a year or so, my uncle moved his family to Greensboro. The fruit stand was growing, and it would soon take both families plus several employees to keep fresh produce for all the people who had begun to drive from all over to buy from us.

Working at the fruit stand wasn't optional for anyone in our family. We all worked there from the time we could bag a pound of candy. I started in the fourth grade. The kids would sweep and haul trash and stack box after box in the back. I spent many hours "running" produce (sorting through a bin of fresh potatoes or other vegetables and fruit to remove the rotten, and I mean gross rotten, things you could find at the bottom). We carried people's groceries to their cars and unloaded the watermelon and cantaloupe trucks, then ate the ones we dropped by "accident." Eventually I was old enough to work behind the scales and the cash register. I worked there Saturdays and summers until my second year in college.

You might say that almost everything I learned about serving people, I learned at Thomas Fruit Stand. With all my heart, I believe those ten years were ordained by God for my training. No one else would have ever thought to start a kid at a fruit stand to prepare her for a life of ministry. I think it was a brilliant call on God's part. I'm sure He knew I needed those lessons very early.

A couple of times a year some people were asked to come from the Blue Ridge Mountains and set up an area to boil molasses. It's a hot, sticky, stinky process. But at the end of the week, Mama would make biscuits and there would be mountain music and the customers loved dropping by to sit around the fire and watch sug-arcane and sorghum become dark molasses. We were mountain people and very proud of the mountain traditions.

Turns out that ministry training doesn't always come from a book or a conference or a pro-fessor. Growing up at the fruit stand was an education all by itself. I was trained by beauti-

I was trained by beautiful moun-tain people with great big hearts.

ful mountain people with great big hearts, most of them without a degree or a pedigree. I bet few had ever traveled outside the state of North Carolina in their lifetime. People should be willing to pay graduate-level tuition to have a fruit stand education.

What I have realized about myself is that I can stand back or hold back or wait too long, when God is in fact asking me to be more like Him. Turns out that I am naturally guarded and hesitant. Not uncaring, just frozen sometimes. When I don't know what to do, many times I have done nothing. Or said nothing. Or given nothing. Other times, I have just lacked follow-through. I meant to, then too much time passed, and I let it go. I realize I can hoard instead of give. I can rationalize instead of being led by the Spirit. I can hesitate instead of obeying.

> Give away your life; you'll find life given back, but not merely given back—given back with bonus and blessing. Giving, not get-ting, is the way. Generosity begets generosity.
>
> —LUKE 6:38 (MESSAGE)

When I catch myself being closed and hesitant, I meekly turn to God and ask, "Do You know that I am really guarded inside? Do You see me hold back instead of giving? I want to be more like You. Make me a woman who can give her heart and her things and her time. Make me generous and remove this shield I hold in front of me."

God has reminded me in this writing that He began teaching me about giving back at the fruit stand. Oh, to live now as a grown-up woman all the beautiful truths I was shown as a child.

Fruit Stand Seminary

Before I knew the books of the Bible in order or the importance of a Greek verb tense, God had begun my seminary training. Most of my character and countenance were shaped at the fruit stand, working alongside my family, completely clueless about the future God had planned and the amazing gift He was giving to me, the daughter of a produce man.

I feel like I should try to dispel any illusion you might have about this fruit stand. I wish I had a picture to show you. It was essentially a long, narrow building made of concrete blocks. The floor was poured concrete. And there were metal garage doors open all along the front and sides of the building when we were open for business. In the summer that meant heat and flies and bees. In the winter it meant that the garage openings were covered with thick plastic that let the light in but did very little to keep the cold out.

The bins for the produce were hand-built by someone a long time ago and obviously used for years before our family took over. Nothing about the look of those bins ever changed. Tomatoes were displayed in a pyramid fashion, precariously stacked on top of one another on the lid of a bushel basket. There were always about eight pyramids of tomatoes out front, and every so often a pyramid would collapse, sending broken tomatoes out into the parking lot. Daddy would pile watermelons outside in the summer and pumpkins in the fall.

Several years ago, I watched a very famous man speaking on television. He conducts "life" seminars around the world with thousands in attendance. I personally know two very successful men who have attended his seminars and would say that weekend changed them forever. I ordered this teacher's twenty-four-CD set so I could learn everything my friends had learned and that changed their lives.

The CDs were good. But what was interesting is that I had already gotten most of his "life coaching" at the fruit stand. The CDs were many old-school lessons I'd learned from the mountain people packaged in a cool, trendy box.

Fruit-Stand Lessons on
Giving Yourself Away

Be Proud of Who You Work For

Every day of my life growing up, I was so proud to be Joe Thomas's daughter. People would say, "Joe Thomas is your daddy? One of the Thomas brothers who owns the fruit stand? Why, he is one of the finest men I have ever known." I'd hold my head a little higher and decide to act like the daughter of a produce man. I wanted to be like my dad.

Every day now, I am still grateful and proud to be Joe Thomas's daughter. But I am even more grateful to work for the Lord God Almighty. I love telling people who I belong to. I can't wait to tell anyone about what God has done for me and for my children. I live to show off the glory of God. Every time I give myself away, I am begging God to glorify Himself. I want to use every act of service and every word I write to change the world for His kingdom purposes.

Saying I am proud to work for God doesn't even come close to the fullness of passion in my heart. As my Texas friend Carlye would say, "I'm eat up."

> But you are a chosen people, a royal priesthood, a holy nation, a
> people belonging to God, that you may declare the praises of him
> who called you out of darkness into his wonderful light.
>
> —1 Peter 2:9

Really Look at People and Listen to Them

When you work at a fruit stand on the side of the road, every kind of person in the world walks in. Professionals came by, but for the most part, most of our customers were hardworking, rural people just like us. When you engage someone with your eyes, stop what you are doing, and commit the work of listening, not only are you giving the gift of hearing, but also the person in front of you begins to feel valuable. For just a moment, you can make someone feel like she matters. We are called to communicate God's value of every person to her. This lesson also goes along with the whole idea that the buyer is always right. In other words, the one you are serving needs to feel like she has been heard. She may actually be as wrong as bruised bananas, but what she needs to say matters.

Be Courteous to Everybody, Not Just the Nice People

When I meet a grumpy person, I try to remind myself of the "maybes" my dad taught me. Every time I have ever been with my dad and a stranger acted rude to us, my dad would always begin with, "Maybe his wife just yelled at him," or "Maybe the last person who came in here was rude to her," or "Maybe no one ever taught that person how to behave." My dad could always imagine someone else's pain and remind me to act bigger than their immaturity.

Sure, some people are just downright mean, but we are called to try anyway . . . up to a point, and then we can follow Jesus' example of what to do if we try and it doesn't work. If someone is repeatedly rude, distant, or unwilling to hear even your most gracious heart of compassion toward them, first, "If it is possible, as far as it depends on you, live at peace with everyone" (Romans 12:18). Next, if they are still unresponsive to your heart like Jesus toward them, then you're done. Shake the dust off your sandals and go the other way (Matthew 10:14). Give yourself away to people who can receive the kingdom of heaven that is within you.

> Therefore, as God's chosen people, holy and dearly loved, clothe yourselves with compassion, kindness, humility, gentleness and patience.
>
> —Colossians 3:12

Never Cheat Anyone

The scales at the fruit stand were the old-fashioned kind. You would put a bag of produce on top and then wait a few seconds for the rolling scale to stop. At whatever the price per pound you read the amount on the red line. That was how much you charged.

After you have weighed thousands of bags of produce, the eye becomes able to judge where the scale will stop before it actually stops. I loved being fast at the cash register, and weighing each bag of produce quickly gave me even more speed. A few times, a customer would think I was too fast and trying to overcharge. I loved reweighing a bag for them and letting them see the actual price on the scale, which was always exactly what I had charged them.

It never pays to cheat anybody for anything. We are called to honesty, even if it hurts or costs us financially or emotionally. Even beyond our calling, God promises to bless our truth-telling.

My daddy never wanted anyone to leave the fruit stand feeling cheated. He'd run out to a family's car and give them a free canta-loupe before he'd let a customer doubt his honesty or generosity.

Sometimes the honest and generous get taken advantage of. I have decided it is the price some of us will pay for doing the right thing. I have given money or things to people who I believe later squandered it. I am sure I have been lied to and taken for a ride many times. I am trying to be smart about my giving, but most times I just have to ask if my heart was good in the gift and leave the rest to God.

> Don't cheat when measuring length, weight, or quantity. Use
> honest scales and weights and measures. I am God, your God. I
> brought you out of Egypt.
>
> —Leviticus 19:36 (Message)

I Am Not Too Good

This wasn't as big a lesson back then as it is now to me. I grew up knowing that I wasn't too good to carry someone's groceries to their car or clean out the trash in the back or ride around in the oldest car in my high school parking lot. I don't think I gave any of it much thought.

But today, I have to remember. I am not too good to serve even the lowliest. I am not too good to take whatever is left or to give my best away or to sleep in a one-star hotel. When I am invited to women's conferences to speak, sometimes I am embarrassed. The host will tell me how difficult other speakers have been with the requests they made and I just want to die. I am the first to tell you that traveling is wearying to both the body and the soul, but none of us, even the most amazing teacher among us, is too good to be nice or to sign someone's book or to say thank you.

We are called to advance the kingdom of God, not the kingdom of me.

> Remember this: Whoever sows sparingly will also reap sparingly, and whoever sows generously will also reap generously. Each man should give what he has decided in his heart to give, not reluctantly or under compulsion, for God loves a cheerful giver.
> —2 Corinthians 9:6–7

Small Things Matter

My grandfather was a tall, stoic man, and we were all on our best behavior when PaPa was near. My grandfather watched his mother burn to death in their house when he was just four years old. My heart breaks every time I remember the story of him standing outside the farmhouse watching while the attempts to save his mother failed. I am sure that's where his solemn personality came from.

At the fruit stand, PaPa was the ever-present produce police. It had to be right, every time. I will never forget walking past him one Saturday afternoon. Evidently I had also walked past some green beans that had fallen to the floor. He called me back. "Angela," he said, without an ounce of emotion, nodding toward the beans, "if that had been a quarter on the floor would you have picked it up?"

"Yes sir," I answered as I reached to pick up the wayward beans. Enough said. He gave me an affirming nod. Lesson learned. I never walked past another piece of produce on the floor. That was like a quarter for my daddy's business.

Small things matter in ministry too. Being mindful of other people's costs. Being faithful when no one is looking. Leaving what you don't need and saving time, money, and energy for other people every time you can.

Jesus told a parable about being faithful in small things. The one who was faithful heard these words:

"Well done, my good servant!" his master replied. "Because you have been trustworthy in a very small matter, take charge of ten cities."

—LUKE 19:17

Working Hard Makes You Feel Better

My cousin Cindy and I were first-rate weekend and summer workers. We were cashiers, produce handlers, fruit basket makers, and all in all did anything they told us to do. I think we played around a lot, but we worked hard too. My friends all had jobs at the mall and I would wave to them from the back of some truck unloading watermelons. We worked hard and came home dirty and tired and hungry.

One of the best things about hard work is that it makes you feel good. Getting tired is a good thing. Physical labor clears your head and gives you immediate accomplishment rewards.

Giving yourself away gives you the same benefit. It just plain feels good to work hard at giving. When one of my kids is down in the dumps or acting selfish and pouty, I will tell him or her to do something for somebody else. It's one of the few things that can lift the fog. To put your burdens on hold and give some time or energy or another gift to someone else makes you feel better too.

Then I realized that it is good and proper for a man to eat and drink, and to find satisfaction in his toilsome labor under the sun during the few days of life God has given him—for this is his lot.

—ECCLESIASTES 5:18

Every Person on the Planet Needs Encouragement

Anyone who knows my dad would tell you that people leave Joe Thomas encouraged, a little challenged, and a whole lot motivated to live great. They have also laughed a bunch and for a few minutes forgotten how hard life is. My dad is so great at encouraging someone to look up and have hope and press on.

When I meet someone, it has become a personal challenge to leave him or her feeling better than when I walked in. Actually, I think that is what the presence of Jesus Christ is supposed to do, and we can do it in many ways. Encourage people. Lift them up. Carry their burdens. Pray. Intercede. Give. Love. Laugh. Anything to be like Christ and point them toward our hope in Him.

Give Some of Everything Away

At the fruit stand you could always count on getting a little extra. Extra attention. Extra service. A hug. A conversation. Lots of laughter. My dad would give an orange to little kids because "when they grow up they'll want to come trade with the man who used to give them oranges." My dad quietly gave food to people who had none and paid the oil bill for customers who told him they were behind. He just gave a little of everything he had, to the church and to us and to his customers.

I have tried hoarding my stuff. And my time. And my heart. It just makes me feel stingy. Giving some of everything is a part of following Christ. When we are aware of where everything comes from, who it belongs to, and why it has been given to us, then it seems foolish to hoard anything that God has given.

> In everything I did, I showed you that by this kind of hard work
> we must help the weak, remembering the words the Lord Jesus
> himself said: "It is more blessed to give than to receive."
>
> —Acts 20:35

Be Fully Present and Enjoy

The fruit stand closed every night at nine. One Saturday night Cindy and I were hurriedly trying to get all the produce in the coolers so we could run home and change, then get to Roy Rodgers along with every other Greensboro teenager who wanted to hang out.

We were being silly and dancing around. Cindy yelled over to me, "Hey, Ang, look at this." Then she broke a curly Mexican green pepper in half and stuck a piece in each nostril so that they were curling out of her nose. I almost died laughing. She was laughing. Then in a moment, panic spread across her face. All that hot pepper juice was now touching the inside of her nose and it was more than awful. She yanked the peppers out, tears started pouring, and not knowing what to do, she ran to the water fountain and started splashing water all over her face. By then she was crying and laughing at the same time, realizing how crazy that idea had been. I think it took her nose a week to recover. Note to the silly-minded, don't ever, ever try that at your local fruit stand. It's been thirty years and we still laugh about it every time we're together.

Oh my goodness, learning to enjoy the present is such a beautiful lesson. When you give yourself away, you have to be present.

> Yes, we should make the most of what God gives, both the
> bounty and the capacity to enjoy it, accepting what's given and
> delighting in the work. It's God's gift! God deals out joy in the
> present, the *now*.
> —ECCLESIASTES 5:19 (MESSAGE)

Don't Take Yourself So Seriously

It's not about you anyway. Nothing about working with rotten produce will give you a head trip. And to keep everything even more humble, there was nothing fancy or new or shiny at the fruit stand. The produce was the art on display. The job and the surroundings were the unassuming backdrop.

In the case of ministry, the worst possible thing we can do is begin to take ourselves too seriously. Jesus Christ is the Savior and we are the backdrop for His glory.

> This most generous God who gives seed to the farmer that becomes
> bread for your meals is more than extravagant with you. He gives
> you something you can then give away, which grows into full-
> formed lives, robust in God, wealthy in every way, so that you can
> be generous in every way, producing with us great praise to God.
> —2 CORINTHIANS 9:10–11 (MESSAGE)

I AM Your God Who Gives

One of the hallmark characteristics of people called to follow Jesus is that they possess the grace of giving. They are not afraid to give themselves and their stuff and their hearts away. In order to reflect the beauty of Christ, they give His light away, and then they give their possessions and their compassion and their energies to be used for His glory. Our God is a giving God. He is gracious, lavish, and good. Oh, that I would be like Him.

I have prayed for many years that God would remove any stinginess still left in me. I am the person who would sneak into the kitchen and take the last piece of cake for myself. I would hoard money and possessions and insignificant things, like toothpaste, for fear of losing all. I would keep back the best for my family instead of sharing the goodness we had been given. But what a complete and total joy it has been to become a giver.

Losing everything has a way of reshaping your heart. When I lost everything and started over after my divorce, I decided to live with open hands. God might move a gift into my hands and just as quickly move that gift from my hand over to someone else. With my hands finally open, the giving was a blessing instead of a struggle. I have come to *love* living inside the grace of giving.

Jesus teaches us to give completely. Living with those same open hands. His call to us includes the call to give mercy (Matthew 5:7), give in secret to those who have needs (Matthew 6:1–4), give our peace (Matthew 10:13), and give freely, just as we have freely received (Matthew 10:8). Paul writes in 2 Corinthians 9:7 that God loves a cheerful giver.

And here is one of the amazing truths of God's calling. What you give for the kingdom, God promises to give back to you. In Luke 6:37–38, Jesus said,

- Give no judgment and you will not be judged.
- Give no condemnation and you will not be condemned.
- Give forgiveness and you will be forgiven.
- Just *give,* and it will be given to you.

Paul expounds on this give and receive principle by saying, "Whoever sows sparingly will also reap sparingly, and whoever sows generously will also reap generously" (2 Corinthians 9:6).

Then Jesus says that what is given back to you will not be just a fraction of what you have given. He says that you will receive bountifully: "A good measure, pressed down, shaken together and running over, will be poured into your lap. For with the measure you use, it will be measured to you" (Luke 6:38).

So, based on the teaching of Jesus and His disciples, we are supposed to give ourselves away like crazy. You've heard it said that you cannot outgive God. I believe that God loves proving that idea true.

My grandmother once told me that a woman came by her house who could not afford to buy groceries for her children. Back then, five dollars would have bought enough to feed a family for several meals. My grandmother decided to give the woman five dollars and some fresh vegetables from her garden. Ma-Ma says that after the lady left she was shocked to realize she had not given her a five-dollar bill but had actually given her a twenty-dollar bill instead. And back then, my grandmother could not afford to give twenty dollars. She says that she prayed and asked God to bless the woman she had given to. And every time she told the story, she was quick to add, "You know I never missed that twenty dollars." God freely gives back to you what you have freely given.

One Reasonable Boundary

Some people hesitate to give themselves away for fear of being taken advantage of. I am absolutely sure that I have been taken for several rides over the years. My compassion was misused. Money I gave was squandered. Some people have taken advantage and then come back to take advantage again. I have decided that my being deceived is not the point. I am supposed to give as I am led by God. How my giving is received is not mine to determine.

But we are supposed to be wise. Our giving is from God's valuable resources through us and we should try our best to use discernment. We should not waste good giving when we know better.

So how much do we give from our wealth or resources? How much do we serve? How much do we invest in a relationship? How much is enough? I have decided that I am supposed to say yes every single time I can.

I love how Eugene Peterson has paraphrased this passage from 1 Peter:

> Most of all, love each other as if your life depended on it. Love makes up for practically anything. Be quick to give a meal to the hungry, a bed to the homeless—cheerfully. Be generous with the different things God gave you, passing them around so all get in on it: if words, let it be God's words; if help, let it be God's hearty help. That way, God's bright presence will be evident in everything through Jesus, and he'll get all the credit as the One mighty in everything—encores to the end of time. Oh, yes!
>
> 4:8–11 (MESSAGE)

May we be women who imitate God, the giver of every good and perfect gift. May our lives be marked by quick compassion. May we live and love simply, without strings, so that people may know the God who is teaching us to be like Him.

Does your heart cry out,
"God, do You know I am guarded inside?"
Then listen as our Lord speaks to you.
God replies to your guarded heart:

DO YOU KNOW WHO I AM? . . .
I AM generous.

I gave My only Son, Jesus, so that you might live. And I mean for you to live a full life underneath My blessing. I AM your God who gives generously. Every good and perfect gift that comes to you is from Me, your Father of Lights. My generosity does not change. It is not like shifting shadows.

I want you to imitate Me. Give and it will be given to you. Give your life away: you'll find life given back, but not merely given back—given back with bonus and blessing. Giving, not getting, is the way. Generosity begets generosity.

Be as generous as I am—give a meal to the hungry, a bed to the homeless, and do it cheerfully. Be generous with the different things I have given to you, passing them around so all get in on it; if words, let it be My words; if help, let it be My hearty help. That way, . . . I will get the credit as the One mighty in everything.

Remember this: Whoever sows sparingly will also reap sparingly, and whoever sows generously will also reap generously. I love a cheerful giver. Share with people who are in need. Don't forget the orphans and the widows. Open your heart and practice hospitality.

You are My beloved and I AM generous to you. Forever and ever, amen.[1]

For we are God's masterpiece.
He has created us anew in Christ Jesus, so we can do
the good things he planned for us long ago.
—EPHESIANS 2:10 (NLT)

CHAPTER TEN

DO YOU KNOW
I AM ORDINARY?

He Is My King and Father

Traveling is my job, but it is also my delight.

This particular weekend, I had been speaking in Phoenix and was catching a flight to Los Angeles. At the same time, my then fiancé, Scott, was flying from North Carolina to California. We were going to spend the weekend with my pastor and friend, Dennis, and his wife, Karen, for our premarital counseling weekend.

In front of me in the security line at the Phoenix airport were two ladies who obviously hadn't flown recently. They were having the toughest time figuring out what to put on the conveyor belt to pass through the X-ray. We started talking and laughing together. I helped them get their shoes into a gray bin. It was a hoot watching these two peel off their layers and take off their jewelry, all the while laughing and complaining to me that it was just too complicated. We had fun and I finally got them through to the other side.

A little while later, I was walking down one of the concourses and I spotted the two ladies riding along on a people mover. They waved and then one of them yelled over to me, "Why you walking? We're riding this thing!"

I yelled back to them across the Phoenix airport, "I'm doing Jenny Craig!"

The one lady yelled back, again, across the entire concourse, "Why you doing Jenny Craig?"

I responded with something akin to a holler, "I'm getting maaarrrieeeddd!"

Well, those two ladies I had never met until security jumped off the people mover and came running to me, dragging their luggage and carry-ons behind them. Both of them, complete strangers, hugged me like I was their lost sister who had just won the lottery for the family. They were thrilled to talk to me. The lead girlfriend said, "Girl, you gotta tell us everything!" Then the questions began. They wanted to know where we met, what he did, how long had I been a single mom. And in the short time I had with those ladies, they gave me more marital advice than I was probably going to get in our entire counseling weekend. Actually, they probably gave me more than I really needed to know.

As we walked along, we discovered we were all on the same flight bound for Los Angeles, so the talking continued as we made our way toward our gate. Somewhere along the way, the more vocal one stopped dead center in the concourse and said, "Wait a minute. Stop right here. I just gotta get something straight. Are you telling me about this man you're gonna marry, that you got four kids and he ain't got no kids, and he still wants you?"

I nodded and squeaked out, "Uh-huh."

Then she said to me, "Girrrllll, that man is blue chip stock," all while she snapped her fingers in the air to add more passionate punctuation.

I laughed out loud and told her that indeed he was.

We traveled together to LAX, and then I walked with my new best friends down to baggage claim. Scott and Dennis were standing there smiling like joy and happiness when we came around the corner. I said to my new girlfriends, "The tall one over there, he's Blue Chip," and they went running. Those two women wrapped him up in more hugging than he may have ever had at one time. I wish you could have seen him. His big six-foot-four frame was surrounded with cute traveling ladies, both of them talking at the same time. He looked out over the top of their heads at me like he was trying to ask, *Who are these two women?*

I just smiled really big and said, "Meet my new best friends."

My pastor, Dennis, said to him, "Just get used to it. Happens everywhere she goes."

I've thought about what those two girlfriends said to me so many times, *"You got four kids and he still wants you?"*

Those words spoke volumes about my heart for at least eight years of my life. I had heard the whispers of Satan loud and clear. And I had my own experiences to go on. I had become certain that no one would ever want me, at least not until the kids were grown. And then, we all still might be too much.

When you are the mom, you are no longer just you anymore, and after my divorce, I knew that I had become five people. That's a lot for anyone to consider. I learned that if I wanted to scare a man away, the quickest way to do that was to introduce myself like this, "Hi, I'm Angela and I have four kids." Bam, that very friendly man instantly had something else to do. And I get it, five of us is a lot.

It's amazing to me that there can be such significance in some areas of your life, but the emptiness always screams louder. Why is that? During those years, I am pretty sure that I was special to my kids. My parents thought I was special. The women at conferences said, "We love you." But what is it with the feminine soul? We can hear beautiful things from people we love and yet ache on the inside for what is missing to make us feel whole, accepted, embraced . . . significant.

What is it with the feminine soul? We can hear beautiful things from people we love and yet ache on the inside for what makes us feel . . . significant.

I am the Bible teacher. I love the Word of God and believe it with all of my heart. I know about longing and loneliness and I truly learned to let it point me toward my Father. But I feel like I have to be honest with you. In my feminine soul, I heard Satan whisper, "No one is going to want a woman like you." I heard him loud and clear. Most days I had enough sense to tell him to shut up. But on the weak days, on the days when the kids had been fussing and the air-conditioning went out for the third time, on days like that, my weary heart would hear the voice of Satan . . . and listen.

I don't know how Satan tells you that you're not special or that you're insignificant, but I imagine he does. Maybe you've heard some whispers like these:

- No one would ever want a woman like you.
- The kids just call you when they need something.
- Your work is so boring, it doesn't matter if you're there.
- You didn't get invited because they don't want you around.
- No one thinks you're interesting.
- Your body is unattractive.
- Your past is too shameful; you can't really be forgiven.
- People like you just get in the way.

Lies. All of them lies. Each one calculated to steal a little piece of your confidence. Each one constructed to make you hesitate. Live a little more reserved. Think less of yourself. Encourage more doubts and lower your self-esteem. Satan is a sneaky one. And just so you're clear on my feelings, I hate him.

I hate what he does to the hearts of women. How he works his schemes against our calling and our purpose. I hate that he can whisper lies into the heart and wound marriages and families. He is a joy-killer. He is the consummate crazy-maker. He is the ultimate discourager, running off with your desire to live, improve, and become.

Satan is the one who cultivates our insecurities. He whispers lies to us and because of our fallen humanity, we lean in and believe him. It's the craziest thing. I really don't know any women who are exempt from his whispering and outright attacks. I do know women who reject him quickly, but no one is isolated from his attempts to discourage.

I am absolutely sure that I am loved. I bet you are loved too, by somebody, somewhere on this planet. And most days that's enough. My life is very full. I love what I do with all of my heart. Like the

T-shirt says, "Life is good." I bet you can point to areas of your life and say, "That is really good," too. Then why, oh why, do so many of us walk around just barely holding back the tears, feeling so very ordinary and plain? Or even worse, feeling rejected and left out.

Many of us could shout to God this very minute, "Do You know I am nothing special down here? Do You know I don't feel like I matter? Do You know how very ordinary I am?"

Our Feminine Discouragement

I think that our feminine varieties of discouragement are much different than the discouragement that happens to men. While the heart is certainly wounded the same, it just seems like different things settle in our souls and steal our joy and our vision. Again, Satan is the author, knowing exactly which script each one of us will read and believe. He comes at us in so many defeating ways, I think we'd do well to consider his ways and learn to respond quickly to the lies.

Unfair Comparison

Good grief, have I been guilty of taking this discouragement path. Several years ago, I was trying to get a book finished, single mom to four children, running the household, mowing the lawn, taking kids to baseball practice, and there were always the never-ending mom surprises, like when you planned a full day, but the school calls you to come and get your sick child.

I said to a friend over coffee, "Why can't I get more accomplished? Why can't I be like so-and-so?"

My girlfriend laughed out loud, "What an unfair comparison. Angela, she does not have any children. Someone cleans her house once a week and three assistants take care of all her details. You only have you."

"Oh, I forgot," I said, and truly, it had never occurred to me that our lives were completely different. I'd just been listening to the whispers, living in a beat-myself-up pit because making my deadlines always seemed like the biggest battle and she could crank out the work. What a goofball I am.

Maybe you've been a goofball too, unfairly comparing yourself to the neighbor down the street or the mom who sits in the bleachers with you at soccer, or the woman you spotted at church who seems to wear a halo over her life.

Believe me, the comparison will only discourage your heart. The whole idea with God is for us to live the lives He has called us to with integrity and passion. I am learning that unfair comparison is a waste of time and energy. I get so much more done when I put my head down and live my own life, not hers.

Anxiety Over Our Children

Last summer we returned from a family trip. My oldest son, Grayson, had been a total teenage grump the entire seven days we had been gone. Nothing big, just all the little stuff that makes it miserable for everybody crammed into one car for a week. When we finally pulled into the garage at our house, Grayson went straight inside and turned on the Xbox. So I very calmly went to where he was and said, "Because you have been difficult to everyone on this trip and chose not to change, I am taking away your privilege. You cannot play the Xbox for two weeks," and I began to unplug the video game.

Grayson looked up at me and said, "Well, I'm going to live with Dad."

I have taken some emotional gut punches, but I will remember that day for the rest of my life. To say that those words came from left field would be the understatement of this century. Weeks of talking and crying and processing ensued, which I'm sure was all very painful for my then fourteen-year-old boy. Then Grayson went to live with his dad and Satan whispered to me, "Look what you have done. You've run him off."

And I know better, but it truly felt like the almost fifteen years in which I had given everything to this person didn't matter anymore. I wasn't special enough. I wasn't a good enough mama. I just wasn't enough. Like I said, I know better and I have much more perspective now. But Satan was so mean to me last summer.

It's been almost a year and Grayson seems to be doing well, but I am ten hours away from my boy and that hurts. He's accumulating his flying miles going back and forth, but his room in our house is much too clean.

The hurdles we face with our children can bring such intimate discouragement and pain. And if we're not careful, we can begin to carry a blame that doesn't belong to us. From the very day this happened with Grayson, my husband said, "Let's trust God to do what's best for Grayson." Arrrgh. Easier to teach that than to live it sometimes.

My friend just called in tears. Her sixteen-year-old Christian boy, the son of a pastor and from a beautiful family, just told her he likes smoking cigars and thinks he'll probably stick with it. After I laughed out loud, we talked about boys being wild at heart and the dumb things they do even when we've taught them better. And though her mama-heart was discouraged and hurting, we decided to trust God together and laughed again over the knotheads we love so much.

Maybe you have a child you are called to trust God for. Don't let Satan whisper his lies of discouragement to you either.

Personal Appearance

I already told you about my extra pounds and the struggle to get back in my old clothes. I keep confessing to my friends, "I am living in sin," because I have great clothes in my closet that are just hanging there. That has to be sin. This past year I have put on the spandex and poured myself into larger sizes, hoping people didn't notice. That would kind of be okay except that my rounder face just happens to be filmed in HD and projected on jumbo screens. I try not to look.

If we're not careful, we can begin to carry a blame that doesn't belong to us.

But oh, what a liar Satan is. What discouragement he gives to many of us with regard to our appearance. The size of our clothes. Hair color and style. The wrinkles on our faces. The tone of our muscles. On and on he shouts and sneers, and over time, even though we try to drown out his taunting, our confidence sinks.

Almost every day finds me in gym shorts and a T-shirt, no makeup and a ponytail, like right this very minute. It's my writing, office uniform. So on those days I don't give all of this much thought. But on the speaking days, yuck. I have to pray it out. Spit on Satan. Remember my place, call on God, and then just go out there anyway. Satan preys on your weakest place. This is one of mine. I've talked to enough women to know this is probably one of yours too.

Social Acceptance

Our family has lived in this new neighborhood and town for almost a year now. A lot of the neighbors came by around the time we moved in. They were all incredibly nice and they brought over sweet things like homemade cookies. They said they were glad we moved in. And we thought to ourselves, *How great to have these nice neighbors.*

That was a year ago. I don't guess we've talked to another one of them since. We wave to them and say hi at the pool. We've even been to knock on their doors, but with bad timing on our part, and we haven't yet found anyone home. Scott and I said to each other last week, "Let's invite them to dinner; it's just about ridiculous that we don't know the people who live close to us."

I honestly think we don't know our neighbors because we all have busy lives and our kids don't go to school together and things like that. But you know how lies start in your mind, *Maybe they know it's us and they don't want to answer the door. Maybe we didn't make the cool neighbor list. Maybe whatever.*

It's all just a scam. A head game. And the worst part is, feeling like we're not special enough to be in the "club" can happen everywhere: in the bleachers, around the community pool, at the kindergarten Christmas party, at church, even in the break room at work.

Last week, my son William had spent the first couple of free summer days with his best buddy, Corey, over here, hanging out, staying up late, and having a great time since school was out. On day three, Corey asked if William could spend the night at his house. I said, "Not tonight. I'm gonna keep Will at home and you guys can have a little break." So Will stayed home. But around 9 P.M. that night, another friend, Jon, called William and invited him to a late-night outing with his church youth group at Celebration Station. They were going to play games from 10 P.M. to 1 A.M. The parents said, "Just let William spend the night since it'll be so late." So we let him go.

You guessed it, Corey found out that William spent the night with a different friend and he was devastated. It felt like we had planned to leave him out, when nothing could have been further from the truth. There was no plan. Just a late-night call. And a mama who said sure. No thinking or plotting or intent to hurt. But Satan told our friend lies. He made him feel like he wasn't special enough to be included.

Satan does the same thing to you and me. Most of the time, no one is plotting or planning or intentionally leaving us out. We must learn to hear God instead.

Real Words of Harm and Hurt

Maybe you have known more than whispers. Someone important has told you that you don't matter. Someone who was supposed to love you violated you. Someone you loved rejected you with hateful words that you remember to this day.

Here is the most important thing I have learned about that kind of awful relationship or the people who wound you with their words—those people don't speak for God.

There was a day, years ago, when a woman I hadn't seen for five or six years called me on the phone. I barely remembered her from a town I used to live in. She spent thirty minutes berating me on the phone with regard to my divorce. She obviously did not know my circumstances nor did she hold a position of friendship or spiritual authority in my life. I still can't believe I stayed on the phone and listened to the crud she gave to me. I offered no answers and made no defense. She didn't deserve either. I just asked if there was anything else she'd like to say, and when there wasn't, I told her goodbye. All I knew at the end of that craziness was that she didn't know me at all and she certainly didn't speak for God.

Vivid Reminders of Our Sin and Its Consequences

I wish we could see forgiveness from God's perspective, and then maybe our past wouldn't keep us in chains. Maybe we would let go of the shame and step into our future. What if we could see that God's forgiveness makes us clean to Him? That forgiveness truly means He remembers no more?

You begin to believe about yourself what you think about yourself, whether it's true or not. And if we continue to listen to the liar, we will just continue to think that what he says of us is true.

I AM Your King and Father

Here is the beautiful, amazing, very very great news: in addition to the fact that God is your King and Father; you are actually the *daughter* of the King. You are a child of God. Truly. Really. Every woman who has asked Jesus Christ to be her Savior has been adopted into the family. Read these words,

> Yet to all who received him, to those who believed in his name, he gave the right to become children of God—children born not of natural descent, nor of human decision or a husband's will, but born of God.
>
> —John 1:12–13

> And by him we cry, *"Abba,* Father." The Spirit himself testifies with our spirit that we are God's children. Now if we are children, then we are heirs—heirs of God and co-heirs with Christ.
>
> —Romans 8:15–17

You are the Father's babygirl. A daughter of the King. I love that. Maybe you just skimmed over that powerful truth. So take a minute. Close your eyes. Take it in. *Daughter of the King. Babygirl of God.*

No matter what this world has been for us, or the lies we have listened to and believed, we must recenter ourselves on this foundational promise of God. We belong to Him. Set apart. Claimed for all eternity. Members of the royal family of God. Daughters of the Sovereign. And everyone knows the daughter of a King is called His princess.

All glorious is the princess within her chamber;
    her gown is interwoven with gold.
In embroidered garments she is led to the king;
    her virgin companions follow her
    and are brought to you.
They are led in with joy and gladness;
    they enter the palace of the king.

—Psalm 45:13–15

One time I read an article in which a woman said she didn't like it when someone referred to herself as a "princess of God." She said it was very self-centered and arrogant. It seemed like the lady who wrote the article was throwing out the truth of Scripture just to preserve her humility. The world has made the idea of princess self-indulgent, but the Bible doesn't waver in its truth. A woman who follows Christ with her life has God as her Father and she has been made a daughter of the King. The daughter of every king who has ever reigned in history is called a princess. The translators of the New International Version of the Bible translate daughter of the King as "princess."

And so, I think we're good. Let us redeem this idea. Just what does it mean spiritually to be God's princess? What does it mean for you and me to take the truth of our position with God and live it out on this earth?

You Are Special

It's so easy to imagine that in God's eyes you are just one of billions. Maybe you believe that most people don't think you are important and so you assume God feels the same way. But God is not like most people. Maybe you even feel like God has favorites. Can I remind you that God is all-powerful. He doesn't need some people more than others. He has no need to play favorites.

But you are a chosen generation, a royal priesthood, a holy nation, *His own special people,* that you may proclaim the praises of Him who called you out of darkness into His marvelous light.

—1 Peter 2:9 (nkjv, italics added)

God uses all of Scripture, the life and death of His Son, Jesus, and the supernatural power of the Holy Spirit to run to your heart because you are so important to Him. His beloved. If we keep rejecting the truth of God's love toward us, that we are special and valuable to Him, we step across the line into a sin of unbelief. It is arrogant to keep telling God that you couldn't possibly matter to Him. He has used all of history to prove to you His love.

Our position as princess comes to us because we have been reborn into the family of God, through belief in Jesus Christ.

> Jesus answered, "I tell you the truth, unless you are born again, you cannot be in God's kingdom."
>
> —John 3:3 (NCV)

> Jesus said, "You . . . have loved them even as you have loved me."
>
> —John 17:23

I have been so privileged to present the truth of who Jesus is and invite women at our conferences to follow Christ as their Savior. When women respond with their hearts, there is nothing I love saying to them more than, "Welcome to the kingdom of God." It is amazing to me that God gives us exactly the same position in the kingdom as His Son, Jesus, but He does!

> And *God raised us up with Christ* and seated us with him in the heavenly realms in Christ Jesus, in order that in the coming ages he might show the incomparable riches of his grace, expressed in his kindness to us in Christ Jesus.
>
> —Ephesians 2:6–7 (italics added)

Your Position as Princess Is Secure

No one can take away the love of God that made you His daughter. Read one of my most favorite passages in Scripture:

For I am convinced that neither death nor life, neither angels nor
demons, neither the present nor the future, nor any powers, neither
height nor depth, nor anything else in all creation, will be able to
separate us from the love of God that is in Christ Jesus our Lord.

—ROMANS 8:38–39

Do you hear what God is saying to you? There is nothing, nothing that you have ever done, nothing that can come to you, no
amount of poor choosing and consequences suffered, no heartache,
no lies from Satan, no abuse, no victimization, there is *nothing* that
can ever separate you from the love of God! And that, my sister, is
the most amazing, very, very great news. Not only has God given
you the same position in His kingdom as His Son, Jesus, but nothing can ever take away His love.

That is the kind of truth you can build your whole life on. God sees
me. He makes me His princess. And He promises that nothing will
ever change His mind or His heart toward me. *You have been given a
great inheritance.*

Praise be to the God and Father of our Lord Jesus Christ! In his
great mercy he has given us new birth into a living hope through
the resurrection of Jesus Christ from the dead, and *into an inheritance that can never perish, spoil or fade—kept in heaven for you.*

—1 PETER 1:3–4 (italics added)

Every princess receives an inheritance she never earned. It's a birth-
right. A gift. A blessing. You and I have been adopted into the blessing
of God's goodness and lavish love toward us. I think the bigger question becomes, "How does a princess of God live in these days?"

To Live Like a Princess

I believe we have been entrusted with a great privilege. As daughters of God we are called to reflect the glorious love of our Father
to this dark and lonely world. If we finally get this amazing truth

worked down into our souls, that *we are so very special to God,*
then we can be the women who change this world, one person, one
encounter, one relationship at a time.

I believe that the privilege of belonging to God is so valuable
that we are to take seriously the pursuit of a princess countenance.
We are supposed to look like members of the family of God. Act
like a daughter of the King would act. Respond like we know who
we belong to and where we are going.

What if you and I chose to aggressively reject the lies of Satan?
Enough years already, he cannot have us anymore. And what if we
stepped into our place as princesses, becoming women who repre-
sent our Father well?

I believe a princess of God is:

- *A woman of the Word.* We should know the family history.
  To whom we belong. His plans for humanity. The calling
  God has for our lives. His purpose in us. And what it means
  to imitate His Son, Jesus.
- *A woman of relationship.* To God and His kingdom on this
  earth. Let us love them well.
- *A woman of grace.* Both to herself and to everyone who
  knows her.
- *A woman of compassion.* The founder of World Vision
  wrote on the flyleaf of his Bible, "Let my heart be broken by
  the things that break the heart of God." May it be the same
  for you and me.
- *A woman of passion.* May we never give up and never run out
  of desire to live for God. Each day, let us renew our strength
  and motivation in the presence of our Father, speaking to Him,
  listening to Him, worshipping His goodness and His glory.

A princess, huh? Not exactly what Satan, the ultimate discourager, wants either of us to believe. Especially not how he wants us
to live. But if I could challenge us both on this one, God paid too
high a price for us to mope around acting like we are not special or
that our lives don't matter.

Maybe your life is a hodgepodge of little pieces. Maybe not one of those pieces all by itself seems too important or special. Maybe you can't point to one thing and say, "That's what I'm good at," or "Hey, there's the special part of me." What we have to get through our thick heads is that our significance is in Christ.

God, our Father, is so wildly and eternally in love with you that He sent His very own "blue chip stock" just for you.

"You mean a God like that knows all about me and still wants me anyway?"

That's exactly what I've been trying to say.

Does your heart cry out,
"God, do You know I am ordinary?"
Then listen as our Lord speaks to you.
God replies to your searching heart:

DO YOU KNOW WHO I AM? . . .
I AM your King and Father.

You are My daughter, My child, and My beloved. You belong to Me. I want you to live like who you are. Live as My beloved. Think as My beloved. Love as My beloved.

The daughter of the King is a princess and you are Mine. I have chosen you and you are special and loved. I know you fully and love you deeply.

There is nothing that can ever come to you that will separate you from My love. My love is eternal. Everlasting. Lavish and good. I promise to keep My promises to you.

You are My princess and I AM your King.
Forever and ever, amen.[1]

They remembered that God was their Rock,
that God Most High was their Redeemer.
—PSALM 78:35

CHAPTER ELEVEN

DO YOU KNOW
I AM BROKEN?

He Is My Redeemer

My family loves to eat with chopsticks.

A few months ago, I took my two girls to a local Asian restaurant for dinner. We studied the menu and were ready to place our order when the waiter came. We made a unanimous decision to split a dish of kung pao chicken with brown rice and bowls of wonton soup all around. The menu said we should choose how spicy we'd like our meal to be; one star was mildly hot and five stars was extremely hot. Our family likes spicy, so we decided to go for it and told the waiter to make it three stars.

After we finished our soup, our waiter brought over the dish of three-star Kung Pao chicken. We eagerly jumped in and began gobbling, or at least as much gobble as you can get with chopsticks. A couple of minutes went by and some kind of delayed heat began to get to all of us at the same time. The food was so crazy spicy that all three of us started gulping water, with tears streaming down our faces. There was no way we were eating three-star kung pao. Someone had obviously dropped all the stars in the kitchen onto our plate.

Through my laughter and tears and nose wiping, I said to the girls, "I think we got way more pao than kung." Then we all lost it again. *More pao than kung.* It's become one of our family's laugh lines. Now we can't eat that dish again without asking the waiter for a little less pao. The waiter never gets our joke, but we always think we are hilarious.

I really wanted to title a book *My Kung Pao Life,* but no one would let me. I told my funny story in a publishing meeting. Everyone laughed and then told me no, that could not be the title. They said a reader in a bookstore would never get it. Evidently, you had to be there.[1]

But I think the whole idea of too much pao is a fairly typical experience for a lot of us. Most of us were just moseying along, ordering a three-star, medium spicy, very safe kind of life, then along came much more pao than anyone could swallow. *Way more pao than kung.* Or at least, that's how it happened for me.

There was a time when I could have been the "good girl" poster child. And truthfully, I wasn't a bit embarrassed about it. I liked being good. There is a high chance I was embarrassingly haughty, but nonetheless, I was plain old good. Afraid of consequences. Fairly boring, I'm sure. I lied to my mama one time about who was driving me home from a restaurant. She found out, and it crushed her to know I had lied to her. That was it for me; I just couldn't lie to my parents, so I didn't. Here's the kicker about being the good girl: I thought it meant life would turn out perfect, or close. You already know the answer to that one. Good is a great option, but it doesn't keep you from the pao that comes from brokenness.

So here I am, a woman who was separated, divorced, lived seven and a half years as a single mom, and just remarried almost a year ago. A broken-down Jesus girl if there ever was one. I have known broken dreams by the hundreds. My children are growing up in a broken home.

Here's the kicker about being the good girl: I thought it meant life would turn out perfect, or close.

And every time I play back these past ten years, I look into the eyes of my beautiful children and it breaks my heart all over again.

This is the place where I could tell you that brokenness has made me a better person, and it has, or I could tell you that my wounds are almost healed, and they are. But my children, my tender, wonderful children, never did one thing to deserve the brokenness they have suffered so early in their lives. This thing has been awful for all of us, but it grieves me that this is my kids' story too. I cry even as I type these words. I am so very, very sorry for their pain and the wounds they carry. I meant for them to have the easy life. They have not.

Just about the time I start to forget what a broken woman I am, someone reminds me: "Well, we won't be able to have another divorced woman speak at our conference." I understand.

"We can't have a divorced woman on the cover of our magazine." Sure, I get it.

"We don't have divorced people on our radio show." It's okay. No problem.

The truth is, I do get it. We're all looking for the answer. We want to read about the ones who got it right so they can show us the way. There isn't one thing about my past that can be changed. I am absolutely sure that God intended for children to be raised by a mom and a dad who love each other and who live in the same house committed to marriage. But that is not my story, nor will it ever be. The question for me has become, given my circumstances and my brokenness, how shall I now live for the glory of God?

An elder at my church said to me, "Angela, Jesus was the Wounded Healer, and I believe that is the ministry He is giving to you." And that is the ministry God *has* given to me. I am so honored to teach the Bible, week after week, all over the world, looking through the lens of my brokenness. It's really okay with me that someone would not have me speak at their event. Truly. Deep down. I promise, I'm very okay. I have such an overwhelming gratitude that God would use me to teach His Word to women that nothing inside of me has time to worry about the places I will never be invited to go.

Most of the emails I receive, the letters I get, and little notes that are slipped to me in the book-signing line are from broken women like me. And every one of them says thank you. Thank you for telling the truth. Thank you for standing up. Mostly they say, thank you for letting God use you. Are you kidding? Thank me? Goodness, I am so thankful to God that He chooses the broken. I will worship Him with my entire life and spend eternity saying to Him, "Thank You for using a woman like me."

What I've come to know for sure is that none of us is spared. We live on this fallen earth, where Satan, the deceiver, plots to steal, kill, and destroy our lives. Maybe your broken heart came a different way than mine, but the likelihood is that you have known a brokenness too.

Maybe you have said to the Lord, "Do You know what a broken woman I am? What in the world can You do with a woman like me?" I have prayed those prayers to God for so many years. It seems like some would want you to believe God can't use broken people. I'm here to testify that God stoops down in His great, great mercy and tenderly raises up every woman who lays her broken life on the altar of His glory.

> *I'm here to testify that God stoops down and tenderly raises up every woman who lays her broken life on the altar of His glory.*

The life of a Christ-follower is not a straight line to glory. There will be twists, turns, stumbles, and downright treacherous roads for each of us. We will not arrive at the end of this journey unblemished and without scars. Not one of us will be able to avoid all the pain or brokenness. But the very beautiful truth we cling to is that glory is our destination.

All throughout Scripture, we see God as our Rescuer, our Redeemer. His ultimate act of redemption came when He sent His only Son, Jesus, to rescue us from the penalty of our sin and redeem our lives from the bondage of sin. Maybe one of the most poignant stories of this same rescuing, redeeming love is found in the book of Ruth.

Ruth and Boaz

The book of Ruth is a series of struggles, brokenness, and redemption, and ultimately, the glory of God. Naomi and her husband had two sons and because there was a famine in their homeland of Judah, they left for Moab. In Moab, Naomi's husband died, leaving her a widowed single mom. The two sons married Moabite women, one named Orpah and the other Ruth. After they had lived there ten years, both of the sons died. Naomi was left without her husband or sons, living with her two now widowed daughters-in-law.

Naomi told the widowed daughters to go back to their families. There was no way she could provide another husband for them and she was returning to her homeland. She told them she would pray for God to give them new husbands some day. Orpah decided to return to her family, but Ruth spoke to Naomi the oath of her commitment. "Where you go I will go, and where you stay I will stay. Your people will be my people and your God my God. Where you die I will die, and there I will be buried" (Ruth 1:16–17).

And so the two widowed women returned to Bethlehem together. Chapter 1 ends with Naomi's bitter grievance toward God, "The Almighty has made my life very bitter. I went away full, but the LORD has brought me back empty. . . . The LORD has afflicted me; the Almighty has brought misfortune upon me" (Ruth 1:20–21).

Almost anyone who has ever suffered so much loss would probably grab at her heart and shake her fist at God. Naomi was no different. Such incredible loss had left her completely empty. Her circumstances felt like an affliction. It even felt like God was the one who had brought misfortune to her life.

Maybe you have known such loss. Maybe your broken heart makes you feel like Naomi, who couldn't find God anywhere in her pain. This story is for women like us who wonder where God is when all hope is gone. It's for the women who wonder where God is when one tragedy after another attacks their faith. And it's a story for women who can't imagine that anything good could ever come from their broken lives.

One thing I want you to keep in mind, in the hardest times, when it seems like everything is falling apart and you're going down holding all the pieces, is that there is always a hidden work of God. When you think that God is distant or that maybe even God has turned against you, I want you to remember that in the unseen, God is plotting for your joy. He is planning the redemption of your brokenness.

After they arrived in Bethlehem, Naomi remembered that she had a relative named Boaz. The Bible calls Boaz a "kinsman-redeemer." Old Testament family law gave the "kinsman" (a close

> *One thing I want you to keep in mind, in the hardest times, when it seems like everything is falling apart and you're going down holding all the pieces, is that there is always a hidden work of God.*

family relative) the right to redeem a relation from slavery or buy back his fields. Another duty of the kinsman, written about in this story of Ruth, is the obligation of the next of kin to marry a childless widow and have a child to carry on the name of the dead husband. In this way, the line of the family would be carried on and the property preserved. Boaz was just the man God had in mind to redeem the broken lives of Ruth and Naomi. He had been working this out in the unseen, plotting for their great, great joy.

As the story goes, Ruth went out during the day to gather fallen grain from various fields, but then "happened" to come to Boaz's field. You're probably already smiling as you realize Ruth didn't just happen onto this godly man's field. God was leading Ruth to exactly where He wanted her to be. Nothing is happenstance with God. Boaz was a kind man who showed favor to Ruth even though she was a foreigner. He instructed his men to care for her and never to harm her.

One night Ruth came and lay at the feet of Boaz while he slept (an Old Testament custom that was intended to signal to a man that the woman at his feet desired him as her kinsman-redeemer). That night, Ruth and Boaz remained pure even though they were alone and spoke to each other with regard to marriage. The next morning, Boaz approached the city elders and with wisdom worked through the process to receive permission to rescue Ruth and the land of her mother-in-law, Naomi.

Eventually, in the most honorable ways, Boaz becomes Ruth's kinsman-redeemer. Ruth takes her refuge underneath the safe, protecting wings of the man who has come to her rescue. He buys all of Naomi's property and takes Ruth as his wife.

> So Boaz took Ruth and she became his wife. Then he went to her, and the LORD enabled her to conceive, and she gave birth to a son. The women said to Naomi: "Praise be to the LORD, who this day has not left you without a kinsman-redeemer. May he become famous throughout Israel! He will renew your life and sustain you in your old age. For your daughter-in-law, who loves you and who is better to you than seven sons, has given him birth."
>
> —RUTH 4:13–16

Boaz and Ruth are blessed with a son they name Obed. And our God, who is always at work in the unseen places, sovereignly placed this beautiful story of redemption in the lineage of Jesus. Obed became the father of Jesse, and Jesse the father of David, and David would continue the direct lineage until the birth of our Savior, Jesus.

I AM Your Kinsman Redeemer

The story of Ruth and Boaz is meant to be a beautiful picture of our relationship with Jesus Christ. You and I have known brokenness in this world. We have suffered loss, rejection, and great disappointment, much like Naomi and Ruth. Each one of us stands in need. Maybe you are like me and a long time ago you realized that you cannot make it through this world in your own strength. You can't figure out how to put all the broken pieces back together. You cannot save yourself from your own sin nature.

So deep is the love of God that He has sent a kinsman-redeemer to buy back our lives from the penalty of death. This kinsman-redeemer's name is Jesus, the very Son of God, sent from the family of God as your "kin." There were four Old Testament requirements for a kinsman-redeemer.

1. *He must be next of kin* (Ruth 2:20). God, our Father, sent His Son, Jesus, who was like us in every way except that He never sinned.

But [He] made himself of no reputation, and took upon him the form of a servant, and was made in the likeness of men: And being found in fashion as a man, he humbled himself, and became obedient unto death, even the death of the cross.

—Philippians 2:7–8 (kjv)

2. *He must be able to redeem* (Ruth 4:4). Jesus assumed our debt, our brokenness, and our sin and paid for it with His life.

For there is one God and one mediator between God and men, the man Christ Jesus, who gave himself as a ransom for all men.

—1 Timothy 2:5–6

3. *He must be willing to redeem* (Ruth 3:13). Oh hallelujah, Jesus was willing to come to this earth to become our kinsman-redeemer. He freely gave Himself to redeem us from our iniquity and to purify us so that we might become the beautiful redeemed of God. I love this truth, that Jesus is the sinner's nearest kinsman.

For even the Son of Man did not come to be served, but to serve, and to give his life as a ransom for many.

—Mark 10:45

4. *He must pay the price in full before redemption could be complete* (Ruth 4:1–6). Speaking of Christ's redemption for us, Ephesians says it beautifully:

In him we have redemption through his blood, the forgiveness of sins, in accordance with the riches of God's grace.

—Ephesians 1:7

All of our debt was completely paid at the cross. All our shame removed. The gift of life eternal was bought back for us by our nearest kinsman-redeemer, Jesus. Do you believe that Jesus is your kinsman-redeemer?

> For all have sinned and fall short of the glory of God, and are justified freely by his grace through the redemption that came by Christ Jesus.
>
> —Romans 3:23–24

To Live Like Ruth

As I've reread this story over and over the past couple of days, I am in awe of several things. First, God is always working in the unseen realm for His glory and to redeem His people, His broken people like me and you. Second, that God would send Jesus to be my kinsman-redeemer takes my breath away. Jesus is our healer, our restoration, and our hope. And third, Ruth was a beautiful role model of godliness for all of us. We could probably spend weeks studying this short little book, but some of the highlights are:

Ruth Was a Woman of Commitment

Ruth's commitment to her destitute mother-in-law is amazing. Ruth turns down the opportunity to return to her own family so that she can stay with Naomi and go to an unknown land as a childless widow. After promising to follow Naomi even to the grave, Ruth also chose to make Naomi's God her own, putting her faith and care in His hands. She decided to live free of the securities of this world and walked with courage toward the unknown.

Though she had lost everything, Ruth moved into her future with such a determined commitment to live with compassion toward Naomi, even through their bleakest times. She took the initiative to provide for them, saying to Naomi, "Please let me glean and gather among the sheaves behind the harvesters" (2:7).

Oh my goodness. Brokenness can make you such a different woman than this. Ruth could still be wallowing in her bitterness and grief. She could have run away from more difficult circumstances to take an easier way out.

If we are to live like Ruth, we can learn to let our broken hearts drive us toward greater commitment and compassion. Committed to love the people God has given us to love with greater passion and responsibility. Committed to be generous with our hearts and our care toward others. Ruth lived as a determined woman. May we do the same. Determine to know God more. Love Him better. Serve the ones He has given. Commit to finish well. Believe that my God who works all things for good will have the final say.

Ruth Worked with Humility

She never presumes it is her right to gather leftover grain (although legally it was); she asks humbly for permission to work in the fields, and then she responds with gratefulness when the permission is granted.

I think brokenness gives a humility we might not have ever known otherwise. The brokenness teaches us that everything is a gift; we are not really entitled to anything. That powerful lesson was woven into the past ten years of my life. When I was a single mom, the kids and I went to zero. We had nothing. Very few possessions. Nowhere to live and no real way for me to earn an income. We were truly a ragtag family and I don't imagine my position in life could have been any more lowly. My brokenness kept me humble back then and reminded me that I wasn't above taking any job the Lord brought to me. Now, all these years later, I still feel that same humility. I am so very grateful, every single day, that God has given this work to me. I try to let everything I do come from that place of humility.

Sometimes people treat me so nicely on the road, I have to stop and remind them, "I came to serve *you*. I'm here to serve the vision you have for this event. God sent me to minister to the women you have invited. This is not the Angela show. I want to minister alongside you and join God in the work He has begun through you."

When ministry comes from a place of humility, the little things keep their perspective, and then it's not inconvenient to meet one more person or do a mike check three times or stand over here, sit over there. Truly, I'm always just happy to be there.

While I am always striving for excellence, working with humility helps me remember my place. Serve. Serve. Serve. God doesn't send me to churches so I can tell the women's ministry director how to do her job better or so I can sit in a little room, alone, until my name is announced. I go to meet people, to worship, to pray together, to teach and to fellowship with the team I am so grateful to have been a part of.

> *While I am always striving for excellence, working with humility helps me remember my place.*

Ruth Was a Very Hard Worker

The Scripture reports, "She went into the field and has worked steadily from morning till now" (Ruth 2:7).

I don't know if it's cool these days to be a hard worker, but I am absolutely sure that it's a character trait God rewards. Remember that the Scripture says, "Whatever you do, work at it with all your heart, as working for the Lord, not for men" (Colossians 3:23).

I think the Lord meant it. He means for us to work at whatever He has given with all our might. It brings Him glory.

Ruth Took Refuge Underneath the Wings of God

Ruth is completely aware that she is a foreigner who is a childless widow. She asks Boaz why he would show favor to her. "At this, she bowed down with her face to the ground. She exclaimed, 'Why have I found such favor in your eyes that you notice me—a foreigner?'" (Ruth 2:10).

Can you hear it in Ruth's tone? She doesn't sound resentful about her circumstances. She is very different from most of the people you run into these days. Most of us expect kindness and feel resentful when we don't get what we think we're entitled to. Ruth is teaching us an entirely different approach. She expresses her unworthiness by bowing her face in humility. She is not proud or arrogant. She is genuinely grateful for the kindness Boaz has shown toward her.

Look at the response of Boaz. He has heard her story from others. Her compassion and commitment have already spoken volumes about her heart.

> Boaz replied, "I've been told all about what you have done for
> your mother-in-law since the death of your husband—how you
> left your father and mother and your homeland and came to live
> with a people you did not know before. May the LORD repay
> you for what you have done. May you be richly rewarded by the
> LORD, the God of Israel, under whose wings you have come to
> take refuge."
>
> —RUTH 2:11–12

I love this more than anything! Ruth models for us the most perfect place to run with our brokenness—underneath the wings of God.

If you are struggling with your broken life or broken heart, run to God. I cannot imagine these past ten years without Him. I have hidden my heart underneath the wings of God. I ran to Him with my shame and my embarrassment, and my heavenly Father took me in. I never sensed any hesitation from Him. I never felt like God thought I needed a spanking. I have only known safety, protection, and refuge underneath the strong arms of God.

Not only have I hidden myself in God, I jumped into the center of His people and stayed there. The people of God have been my family. They prayed for me and strengthened me when I did not have strength on my own. So often, they came or called "because God led" them to. He used so many to care for me and the children. An elder in my church let us rent very cheaply a house that he owned. This act was a modern-day version of allowing me to gather leftover grain from his fields.

I will never forget a woman I barely knew speaking to me at church. She said, "I know where you live. Right on the corner of Ebenezer Road. I drive down that road all the time, and I just wanted you to know that when I drive past, I pray for you and your children." Do you realize how much that meant to me? God, my refuge, had directed strangers to pray for me.

Maybe today, you need the refuge of God. And if you do, I'd love to take you to Him. Maybe you can do something like this.

Get to a space where you can lie on your face. Really, just lie on the floor somewhere quiet. Your bedroom, the living room. If you're in a hotel room, throw down some towels and lie there before God. There is a reverence about humbling yourself before God with your body.

Maybe the minute you lie down and the room grows quiet, you will sense it; God is present. I pray that the first thing you feel in your soul is the overwhelming, enduring love of God.

Then maybe you can pray something like this: "God, I need to hide myself underneath the wings of Your love. Please be my hiding place. Would You protect me and heal me and begin to put all my pieces back together?"

And keep praying, from the inside out. Begin with all the ache inside your heart. Hide those hurts and longings with God. He is able to keep us safe. He is able to heal. And He will do more, according to Joel; He will restore all that the locusts have eaten. As you keep praying out, begin with your soul, then move onto your physical body, the people who are closest to you, relationships and circumstances that relate to you. Just pray your life over to God.

Now receive. Lie still and listen for God. Let Him minister to your tender heart.

Ruth Chose Righteousness and Integrity

Sometimes when we're suffering, the idea of running away seems tempting. Everything becomes too much for one woman to carry and we can be tempted to say, "Forget it. I quit. I'm tired of trying to live right or do right. This all keeps hurting with the same repetitive pain. I'm outta here." I'd be lying if I didn't tell you that many times I thought about running away. We sponsor four kids in South Africa and I can't tell you how many times I told the children,

"We're going to Africa. They need us over there." Other days, when the frustrations were milder, I'd tell them, "We're moving to Montana and I'm gonna be a café waitress." When you are so awfully broken, starting over somewhere anonymous sounds perfect.

In the depths of those dark days, I also began to understand why men and women do stupid things when they're hurting. I think it's one part distraction from the pain and the other part longing to feel a little pang of anything that mimics love. They choose a momentary diversion and lose their integrity. Satan schemes an alluring trap for the broken, but the devastating catch is that living without integrity only leads to more brokenness and pain. I have watched it happen all around me.

Rather, you are called, like Ruth, to run to God as your refuge and then live with integrity, even if you are right in the middle of the hardest days you have ever known. Stay with God and keep choosing right. I mean it. Do whatever you have to do to live a clean, right life. Honestly, if you live right toward God and man, then who can have anything on you? No one, that's who. They may gossip about you, but they can't have you, because you're clean! Circumstances may line up against you, but they will not overtake you, because you are a woman of integrity. If I could imprint one *huge* idea on the heart of every woman, I think this one thing would radically change our lives, our families, and our communities. Just live right. All the time. In every choice. With all people, even the ones who've done you wrong.

Ruth chose commitment, humility, hard work, the refuge of God, and integrity. May it be the same for you and me!

My Boaz

On my wedding day, a rainy Saturday afternoon, June 14, 2008, God who is my Redeemer sent a Boaz to love me and my children. William Scott Pharr stood under a tent and watched me and my dad trip over the tent stakes with our umbrella, make a joke for the crowd, and then make our way down the aisle behind my daughters. A stringed ensemble played something beautiful and all our friends sat happily in their garden chairs, but all I could see was the best man I have known on this earth, waiting for me. My boys stood beside Scott in handsome tuxedos and the girls were beside me, dressed in white. This man was marrying our family and I wanted the children to understand the power and the reverence of those moments. I wanted everybody dressed up to celebrate the commitment we were making and the holiness of our vows.

Our pastor, Rob Taylor, led us in the most beautiful order of service. The children each read passages of Scripture. Our parents came to lay hands on us and join the pastor in prayer. My friend Kim Hill sang The Lord's Prayer over our families. Scott and I exchanged vows and rings. But perhaps the thing that everyone will remember about that day is when Pastor Rob said to Scott, "Are you ready to say your vows to your children?"

Then Scott turned toward them and read the vows he had written,

"Taylor, Grayson, William, and AnnaGrace,
I Promise:
To love your mother,
To love and respect you,
Guide and nurture you
Be patient and kind,
To listen and support you,
Protect you,
To help you follow your dreams,
To cherish our time together,
To show you every day the joy you bring to my life,
To be a reflection of God's love in your life,
And to love you unconditionally forever."

No one under the tent could breathe. Me especially. Who could send a man to love a single mom and her four kids? God, who is my Redeemer. Who could give a man such a deep love for children who are not his own? God, my Redeemer. Who has knit our hearts and our home together, to this very day? God who is our Redeemer.

────────────── ❀ ──────────────

Does your heart cry out,
"God, do You know I am broken?"
Then listen as our Lord speaks to you.
God replies to your tender hear:

DO YOU KNOW WHO I AM? . . .
I AM your Kinsman-Redeemer.

I AM the one who redeemed you through Christ Jesus. I've released
you from bondage. I've loosed you from your prison. I predestined
you to be Mine, and those I predestined I called; and those I called I
have justified; and those I justified are also in My sight already glori-
fied. No one can bring any charge against you and make it stick. I am
the God who justifies and redeems.

No matter what kind of brokenness you have known or what bit-
terness has come to you, I AM the God who heals. I have sent My Son,
Jesus to be your healer and your redeemer.

I AM working in the unseen for your restoration. Let Me hide you
underneath My wings of protection. I AM near to the brokenhearted.

You are My beloved and I AM your redeemer.
Forever and ever, amen.[2]

May the God of hope fill you with all joy and peace
as you trust in him, so that you may overflow
with hope by the power of the Holy Spirit.
—ROMANS 15:13

CHAPTER TWELVE

DO YOU KNOW
I AM DISAPPOINTED?

He Is My Hope

Sometimes we forget about hope.

I'll never forget sweet Donna Stewart from Hattiesburg, Mississippi. She and her girlfriend picked me up from the Jackson airport a few years ago for a weekend at their church. On the hour's drive over to their town, I was riding along in the backseat, answering their questions and telling my single-mom stories. One of them asked me, "Angela, do you think you'll ever remarry?"

Goodness, I launched into a long, prewritten narrative telling them all the reasons I'd probably never remarry. *The kids were my life and total focus. I had a lot happening. The ministry.* On and on I went, and Donna listened ever so kindly.

You probably already know what I'm getting ready to tell you. That long narrative I rattled off was a cover. It was a cover for all my hurt. It was the story I told to hide my sadness. It was the kind of thing a woman might say to mask her disappointment. The truth was I had come to believe there wasn't a man (at least a single, godly, fun man) who would come for me. I was learning the very real lesson that every single day, God was all I needed. He would have to be enough. I had been forced to surrender to God as my fullness and my portion.

But Donna obviously read right through my disappointment and my babbling. At the next stop, she turned around to look at me and then firmly but graciously asked, "Angela, would you leave the door open for God?"

Every time I see Donna's smiling face, I tell her, "Thank you." From her years of wisdom and similar circumstances, Donna spoke deep into my spirit that day as we drove along a rural Mississippi road, "Would you leave the door open for God?" What about you? Would you leave room for hope? For the miraculous? For what God has beyond anything you dream for yourself?

As I write to you this afternoon, Scott and I are a few days away from our one-year wedding anniversary. Hallelujah! Thank you, Donna, for the strong persuasion about the door I had passed by, the God of Hope door.

Sitting perched on my bed, with laptop on my knees, I just said to the Lord again, "Thank You. Oh, thank You so very much." And almost immediately it was if the Holy Spirit asked me, "Where else do you need to keep the door open for God?" Instant tears just burst out of me, and the list, this huge list of pain and sadness, has swept through me. A list of this-very-day disappointments that makes my spirit ache and grieve.

- My son who lives too far away.
- My mom with ovarian cancer.
- My brother-in-law with thyroid cancer.
- My nephew Cole, and his daily struggles to grow up.
- My brother's great heartache and sadness.
- My single-mom girlfriend with four boys and not one person in this world to help her.
- The sister I wish I'd gotten to know.

Maybe a list of disappointment rushes out of you too. I haven't cried like I just did in such a long time. Life just keeps coming, doesn't it? One part resolves and then there is all the rest to remember to open the door for.

I believe God knows. I am sure of it. And because of His tender mercy, He receives me when I pray.

God, do You know there is disappointment all around me? So much. Too much. Do You know how we ache with sadness and grieve what is not turning out right? Oh Lord, please hear us all, each one of us who had hoped for more and struggles every day with this flawed world and the brokenness it brings. Amen.

The Bible and the Disappointed

Scattered all through the Scriptures are people much like us, men and women who have experienced unfulfilled expectations. Leaders who failed. Disciples who doubted. Prophets who felt abandoned. Women who longed for children.

Moses was disappointed by the grumpy people he led and by his ultimate failure. He led the nation of Israel to the Promised Land and then wasn't allowed to enter. The Lord even told Moses not to talk to Him about it anymore.

But because of you the LORD was angry with me and would not listen to me. "That is enough," the LORD said. *"Do not speak to me anymore about this matter.* Go up to the top of Pisgah and look west and north and south and east. Look at the land with your own eyes, since you are not going to cross this Jordan. But commission Joshua, and encourage and strengthen him, for he will lead this people across and will cause them to inherit the land that you will see."

—DEUTERONOMY 3:26–28 (italics added)

David was a great victor over Goliath, and then King Saul became jealous of David's popularity, so the giant-killer had to run for his life and live like a fugitive for about ten years. David's discouragement was so acute that he thought God had vanished. And from his deep discouragement (read the book of Psalms), David did things that were wrong and foolish.

Despite all of David's recklessness and foolish behaviors, God kept His promise and made him king of the nation of Israel. Look at what David wrote after God kept His promise, in His own time and in His own way:

I love you, O LORD, my strength.

The LORD is my rock, my fortress and my deliverer;
my God is my rock, in whom I take refuge.
He is my shield and the horn of my salvation, my stronghold.

I call to the LORD, who is worthy of praise,
and I am saved from my enemies.

—PSALM 18:1–3

And then there were the disciples. Can you imagine the devastation for Jesus' disciples? They had believed He was the Messiah. They had left everything to follow Him and then expected they would usher in the kingdom alongside Him. Instead, He was crucified and buried. And all their hopes were buried in the tomb with Him. God had a bigger plan. Jesus had to die and rise again to rescue all of humanity from the bondage of sin.

Disappointment is not a new, modern-day plight. Its sorrow has come to all people of every generation. Men and women, young and old, the wise and the foolish, the carefree and the meticulous. We have all known disappointment, sadness, and loss. No one is exempt. No one is immune. I believe God knows our predicament. He understands our humanity. I think we'd do well to spend our time deciding what to do with the inevitable.

What is a woman to do with her disappointment and her very real struggles with sorrow? People and our relationships disappoint us. Circumstances cause us sadness and regret. This one thing I know for sure, we can run to Jesus. He alone is the answer. He alone is our hope.

The Stories of Two Daughters in Need

In the fifth chapter of the book of Mark, we find the stories of two different daughters. One is the daughter of Jairus, who is twelve years old and desperately sick. The other is a grown woman, called "daughter" by Jesus, who for twelve years has been suffering an affliction of bleeding.

Before we jump into this passage, I just have to tell you, I love the Bible so much! I love the intentional method in the writing and emphases God gives so that maybe we won't miss it. And then there is the beautiful testimony of three gospels, Matthew, Mark, and Luke, that all record these miracles. Three times, the same account. Maybe we will three times more consider their truth for our own lives!

There are two daughters. Two in great need. Two who are desperate to be healed and without any other hope. But notice the contrasts as we read through this story.

They come to Jesus in different ways. The first has a father who is a bold, important member of the synagogue. The second one is timid and unknown.

The Scripture wants us to see two different versions of twelve years. The first daughter has given her father twelve years of happiness. The second woman has an affliction that has given her twelve years of sorrow.

Jairus, the father of the first, was a wealthy man, but his wealth could not save his dying daughter. The second woman had spent everything she had to find a cure, yet no doctor had been able to help her.

Each of the daughters receives life from the only One who can give it to her. I can't wait for you to read these two stories woven together so that we might see God more clearly.

Here is the story of the first daughter and her need.

When Jesus had again crossed over by boat to the other side of the lake, a large crowd gathered around him while he was by the lake. Then one of the synagogue rulers, named Jairus, came there. Seeing Jesus, he fell at his feet and pleaded earnestly with him, "My little daughter is dying. Please come and put your

hands on her so that she will be healed and live." So Jesus went
with him.

—Mark 5:21–24

Do you notice how the father, Jairus, came boldly to Jesus? He
was synagogue leader, and he wasn't afraid to come right up to
Jesus and begin pleading for the daughter he loved. He rushed to
see Jesus, the last hope and only hope he had for his suffering child.
Now read about the second daughter,

A large crowd followed and pressed around him. And a woman
was there who had been subject to bleeding for twelve years. She
had suffered a great deal under the care of many doctors and had
spent all she had, yet instead of getting better she grew worse.
When she heard about Jesus, she came up behind him in the
crowd and touched his cloak, because she thought, "If I just touch
his clothes, I will be healed." Immediately her bleeding stopped
and she felt in her body that she was freed from her suffering.

—Mark 5:24–29

Do you see how this daughter came to Jesus? Timid. Shy. Having
done everything else she could think to do. Can you imagine the
pain and constant fatigue that must have plagued this woman every
day? What a burden she carried. She had become increasingly sick
through the years. Probably ashamed.

Bleeding for twelve years would have kept her unclean according to religious laws and removed her from the community. In spite
of all her embarrassment, I love that she was just as determined
to get to Jesus. In direct contrast to Jairus, who ran to Him, this
woman anonymously pushed through the crowd and sneaked up
behind Jesus to touch her finger to the hem of His robe.

Though her approach was entirely different, her need for healing was the same. She could have let any number of thoughts keep
her from the only hope she had. I'm sure she could have told herself, "I am not important enough to ask Jesus for help," or "Look,
He's already going with Jairus to his house." Maybe she could have

thought, "Nothing else has worked. Why should I even try?" This woman had exhausted every hope and all her money. She knew there was no deliverance from her suffering apart from Jesus, so she laid aside the excuses and came in faith to Jesus. He was her last hope, too, and her only hope for healing.

At once Jesus realized that power had gone out from Him. He turned around in the crowd and asked, "Who touched my clothes?"

> "You see the people crowding against you," his disciples answered, "and yet you can ask, 'Who touched me?'"
> But Jesus kept looking around to see who had done it. Then the woman, knowing what had happened to her, came and fell at his feet and, trembling with fear, told him the whole truth. He said to her, "Daughter, your faith has healed you. Go in peace and be freed from your suffering."
>
> —Verses 31–34

Despite her fear and even with her low opinion of herself, Jesus noticed her. He called her to Himself. He called her "daughter." He could have let her drift back into the crowd, but He didn't. I think Jesus wanted this woman to receive more than a physical healing. He wanted her to be noticed. To publicly receive His tenderness. To publicly hear Him call her "daughter." I think He wanted to minister to her spirit so that she would know Him as Savior.

> While Jesus was still speaking, some men came from the house of Jairus, the synagogue ruler. "Your daughter is dead," they said. "Why bother the teacher any more?"
> Ignoring what they said, Jesus told the synagogue ruler, *"Don't be afraid; just believe."*
> He did not let anyone follow him except Peter, James and John the brother of James. When they came to the home of the synagogue ruler, Jesus saw a commotion, with people crying and wailing loudly. He went in and said to them, "Why all this commotion and wailing? The child is not dead but asleep." But they laughed at him.

After he put them all out, he took the child's father and
mother and the disciples who were with him, and went in
where the child was. He took her by the hand and said to
her, *"Talitha koum!"* (which means, "Little girl, I say to you,
get up!"). Immediately the girl stood up and walked around
(she was twelve years old). At this they were completely
astonished.

—VERSES 35–42, (italics added)

Can you imagine the devastation of Jairus when his friend came
to tell him, "Your daughter is dead"? I can see him doubled over
in sorrow, immediately overtaken with the great grief that would
come to any parent.

And then came the strong words of Jesus to Jairus, "Don't be
afraid; just believe." Jairus had to make a decision, whom to believe? His friend who came with sad news or the One he had put
his hope in.

When Jesus and Jairus arrived at his house, the professional
mourners had already been called and, in their tradition, they were
standing outside weeping and wailing loudly. The presence of the
mourners was proof that the girl was actually dead. The family
would have never called them if there had been the slightest chance
the girl was still alive. But then the Lord of Hope spoke: "The child
is not dead but asleep." Pay attention to the unbelieving—they
laughed. Unbelief laughs at God's
Word, but faith leaves the door
open and watches for the power of
God.

> *Unbelief laughs at God's
> Word, but faith leaves the
> door open and watches for
> the power of God.*

Without great spectacle or fan-
fare, by His authority as the Son
of God, Jesus healed the daughter who had been suffering and
returned life to the daughter who had been dead. Two daughters, two lessons of hope. May we see in these that the loving
God of heaven, our divine Creator and Lord, is our hope and our
salvation.

When Disappointment
Becomes Despair

Disappointment can become a progressive sadness. What begins as mild sadness and loss has the ability to grow and snowball in our lives. Maybe you find yourself somewhere past disappointment. Look at the progressive D's in order:

1. Disappointment
2. Discouragement
3. Depression
4. Despondency
5. Despair

Disappointment is the first little seed that can distract our faith. It sounds so harmless to say, "I'm disappointed," but that struggle can be the tip of progressive heartache that stops spiritual growth, making us live bitter and defeated lives.

I'm sure you know someone who began with disappointment, but then year after year progressed, heartache after heartache, and he found himself ultimately in a desperate pit of despair.

I know a woman who is teetering on the edge of despair. She has walked with God, but her journey has been so very disappointing. A divorce several years ago left her alone with five children, living just a couple of dollars above poverty. The loss of her parents, each with long and suffering cancers. The rebellion of her children. The everyday, thundering anger of her ex-husband, his ugly messages, his irresponsible actions, and his verbal attacks toward the children. She goes to work every day. And prays to be loved. And agonizes over her children. And what began as disappointment so many years ago has accumulated and mushroomed in her heart. Now the ugliness of despair threatens to close her in with its darkness. My sweet friend needs the hope of God.

What I want you to know is that no matter where life may have taken—you, disappointment, depression, or even despair—the answer for our souls is ever the same. Run to Jesus. Some circumstances will never change. We have to learn to accept them and keep trusting God in spite of our disappointment. Push through everything that crowds round your heart. Get next to Him. Go boldly to Him. Be determined in your need and even in your shame. Jesus is the answer.

> Though the fig tree does not bud and there are no grapes on the vines, though the olive crop fails and the fields produce no food, though there are no sheep in the pen and no cattle in the stalls, yet I will rejoice in the Lord. I will be joyful in God my Savior.
> —Habakkuk 3:17–18

Mike Feazell writes:

> Jesus doesn't care who you are. He doesn't care if you're timid and shy, young or old, a leader or an outcast. He knows you, loves you, cares about your needs and fears and crises, and is ready to help. He listens to your up-front, head-on pleas and he senses hopeful hearts at the back of the line and behind the door. Your personality, your temperament, your status, nor even (especially) your sinful history can erect a barrier he can't bring down like the walls of Jericho.[1]

Run to Jesus, my sister. In our disappointment, there is only One place for us to find hope.

I AM Your God of Hope

Most people understand hope as wishful thinking, as in "I hope something will happen." That is not what the Bible means by hope. The biblical definition of hope is "confident expectation." We, the followers of Christ, have set our confidence firmly on the power and promise of God. We expect that He will be sovereign in our lives. We expect that He is working all things for good and for His glory. We can rest and find our hope in the "confident expectation" that our loving God is completely and eternally in control.

The psalmist had learned that when you have nothing left but God, you realize He is enough and even more than enough. He is our hope and our refuge.

> Yet I am always with you;
>   you hold me by my right hand.
> You guide me with your counsel,
>   and afterward you will take me into glory.
> Whom have I in heaven but you?
>   And earth has nothing I desire besides you.
> My flesh and my heart may fail,
> but God is the strength of my heart
>   and my portion forever. . . .
> But as for me, it is good to be near God.
>   I have made the Sovereign LORD my refuge.
>
> —PSALM 73:23–26, 28

For the woman who struggles with disappointment or even worse, here is the hinge upon which this whole truth turns. We will have to consciously go to the source of hope. We have to go to Jesus. Jairus ran to Him boldly. The ailing woman went meekly. But each went with a determined faith to get to the only hope they had. You and I will have to do the same.

When fresh disappointment washes over you—go to Jesus.

When old pain resurfaces to remind you of your loss—go to Jesus.

When circumstances look bleak and there is no visible way—go to Jesus. We must learn to trust the God of the unseen for what is yet to be revealed. Listen to Elisha teach about hoping in what we cannot yet see.

> "Oh, my lord, what shall we do?" the servant asked.
>   "Don't be afraid," the prophet answered. "Those who are with us are more than those who are with them."

And Elisha prayed, "O LORD, open his eyes so he may see."
Then the LORD opened the servant's eyes, and he looked and saw
the hills full of horses and chariots of fire all around Elisha."

—2 KINGS 6:15–17

God's protection and provision were there all along, even though the servant could not see them. The same holds true for us as believers. Those who are with us are more than those who are against us. I pray right now that we will trust God, who is with us, more than the circumstances that face us. I am asking God to open our eyes so that we can see who He really is and the powerful protector He promises to be.

A Woman of Hope

You know her when you meet her, because there is no denying when you have encountered a woman of hope. First, there is her countenance. The irrepressible countenance that belongs to the woman who sets her heart on the hope of God.

My grandmother, Ima, was such a woman of hope. The Spirit of God danced all about her. You could see it in her eyes. You heard it in her voice. And in her great, big, ever-present laughter. Nothing, and I mean nothing, stole her joy. I stood with her at funeral homes, in the kitchens of the sick and grieving, and watched that woman walk in with the real hope of God to every circumstance and every situation. Most of the time, she could see what God was up to (now we call that quality discernment), and she trusted even when she couldn't see.

Because her hope was so firmly placed and her confident expectation never wavered, my grandmother was a beautiful combination of reverence and fun and silliness. I don't think she ever doubted God one moment in her life and probably had the best time on this earth because of it. Hope will do that, you know. Hope stands up the downtrodden and brings light into the eyes of believers. Hope puts a song in your heart and a kick in your step. My grandmother had all of that.

The story goes that my grandfather bought a new record-playing stereo. I can see it in my mind, taking up most of the corner in their kitchen with a crocheted doily and framed photos on top. My grandmother was in the kitchen making dinner, while Grandpa sat with the guests in the living room. The stereo wasn't playing but Ma-ma was singing and carrying on, entertaining herself while she made chicken and dumplings, I'm sure. Frustrated with all the loud noise coming from the kitchen, Papa said to the guests, "Guess I'm gonna have to get that stereo fixed. Sure does make an awful racket."

What I loved about my grandmother is that she didn't care if it was an awful racket. It was your loss for not getting in on all the joy.

Last year around this time, God called my grandmother home. I'm sure Pa-pa was waiting for her by the nearest gate, where he could hear her hollering and singing before she was even in sight. The night of visitation at the funeral home, my family stood in line for hours, greeting all the people who had loved my ma-ma. No one came to us in tears. They all knew that Ima was certain of her hope and her eternity in heaven. They all knew heaven was a little more fun now that she was there.

Toward the end of the night, a very elderly woman with a cane made her way around to each of the family members. The last person she spoke to was my daughter Taylor. The frail woman, who was probably older than Ma-ma, leaned in and took Taylor by the hand. "Honey, I'm so sorry for your loss. Ima was one of the most beautiful people I've ever known," she said with great meaning.

"Thank you so much," Taylor responded as she had all night.

Then the spry old lady, with her obligatory words complete, leaned a little closer so Taylor could hear, "Now, I gotta get outta here. *American Idol* comes on at eight o'clock and I ain't never missed a one of 'em."

Taylor smiled at the lady and then turned to laugh out loud while she tried to tell us all what just happened. The whole family thought Ma-ma would have loved that. No need for long-term grieving when you know where your hope is. Besides, Ma-ma felt exactly the same way about *The Price Is Right*.

According to the Bible, many benefits and blessings come to the woman who chooses hope.

Hope gives us joy and peace.

> Now may the God of hope fill you with all joy and peace in believing, that you will abound in hope by the power of the Holy Spirit.
>
> —Romans 15:13 (nasb)

Hope ushers in the goodness of God.

> The Lord is good to those whose hope is in him, to the one who seeks him.
>
> —Lamentations 3:25

Hope gives us protection.

> Behold, the eye of the Lord is on those who fear Him, on those who hope for His lovingkindness.
>
> —Psalm 33:18 (nasb)

Hope gives us strength, courage, boldness.

> Be strong and let your heart take courage, all you who hope in the Lord.
>
> —Psalm 31:24 (nasb)

Hope gives us confidence for this life and our callings.

> For it is for this we labor and strive, because we have fixed our hope on the living God, who is the Savior of all men, especially of believers.
>
> —1 Timothy 4:10 (nasb)

And so, my dear sister, I pray you are getting to know the character of God. Oh, how I want you to know Him more. How I pray that every weakness and insecurity, every disappointment and frailty will drive you deeper into the knowledge of our blessed God.

Do you know who He is?

He is worthy.
He is your comfort.
He is the God Who Sees.
He does not grow weary.
He is your sufficiency.
He is your Savior.
He is here.
He is your strength.
He is generous.
He is your King and Father.
He is your Redeemer.
He is your hope.
He calls you His daughter and treats you as His own.

And, hallelujah, our precious God is your hope.

No matter what, will you remind one another to leave the door open for God? Will you become a woman of great and abundant hope? May we all grow in this grace. Lavish. Bountiful. Overflowing.

Let us swing open the doors of our hearts to His great truth. Unlock the front doors, the back doors, the cellar doors, and the secret doors no one has ever seen.

Don't stop there.
Throw open the windows.
Turn the porch light on.
Open the locked gate.
Clear the path to your heart.

Do everything you can to leave the door open and then make sure that you watch for God. When Hope walks in, He'll take your breath away. Your darkness will be dispelled by His light. The joy of His Hope will fill the emptiness of your heart and put a song in your mouth.

And right there, wrapped in the glorious Hope of our Lord and Savior, you can rest, my sister. It's time to rest. Let the peace of God transcend your understanding. You are known. You are loved. You are rescued. You are safe. For now and forever, amen.

―――――――――――― ✿ ――――――――――――

Does your heart cry out,
"God, do You know I am disappointed?"
Then listen as our Lord speaks to you.
God replies to your discouraged heart:

DO YOU KNOW WHO I AM? . . .
I AM your God of hope.

When you feel forgotten, I AM your hope. When your spirit is downcast, I AM your hope. When your soul faints, I AM your hope.

I AM unfailing. I AM full redemption for your life. I AM your promised hope for eternal life. My Son, Jesus, is your living hope.

You can put your confidence in Me so that you do not have to fear disappointment and failure. You can believe that I keep My promises and rest in the faithfulness of My everlasting hope. Put your trust in Me and receive My blessing. My hope does not disappoint.

I pray that the eyes of your heart may be enlightened so that you can know the hope to which I have called you. Faith is being sure of what you hope for and certain of what you cannot see. Hold unswervingly to My hope.

Let your heart be glad. Let your soul rejoice. My hope is an anchor for your soul, firm and secure. In the light of every disappointment and suffering, I AM your everlasting hope.

You are My beloved and I AM your hope.
Forever and ever, amen.[2]

NOTES

INTRODUCTION
1. J. I. Packer, *Knowing God* (Downers Grove, Ill.: InterVarsity Press, 1973), 41–42.

CHAPTER ONE: DO YOU KNOW I AM AFRAID TO DREAM BIG?
HE IS WORTHY.
1. D. A. Carson, *New Bible Commentary: 21st Century Edition,* 4th ed. (Leicester, England; Downers Grove, Ill., InterVarsity Press, 1994), Matthew 24:36.
2. See Revelation 4:11; Psalm 19:1; Deuteronomy 10:17; 1 Chronicles 29:11; Job 13:11; Psalm 29:4, 96:6; Hebrews 1:3; Psalm 145:3.

CHAPTER TWO: DO YOU KNOW I AM INVISIBLE?
HE IS MY GOD WHO SEES.
1. James 1:17.
2. Ephesians 1:18.
3. See Genesis 16:13; 2 Chronicles 16:9; Job 28:24; Job 34:21; Psalm 33:13–15; 139; 34:15; Psalm 121.

CHAPTER THREE: DO YOU KNOW I AM TREMBLING INSIDE?
HE IS MY COMFORT.
1. Hannah Whitall Smith, *The God of All Comfort* (Westwood, N.J.: Barbour, 1984), 27–28.
2. W. W. Wiersbe, *Wiersbe's Expository Outlines on the New Testament* (Wheaton, Ill.: Victor Books, 1997), 476.

3. W. W. Wiersbe, *The Bible Exposition Commentary* (Wheaton, Ill.: Victor Books, 1996), 2 Corinthians 1:3.
4. Smith, *The God of All Comfort*, 34.
5. See 2 Corinthians 1:3–5, Isaiah 66:13; John 14:27; Isaiah 51:12–13; John 3:16; Isaiah 61:1; Psalm 34:18; Matthew 5:4; Isaiah 57:18; Ephesians 3:18; 2 Corinthians 7:6; John 14:16; Psalm 71:21; Psalm 94:19; 2 Thessalonians 2:16–17; Jeremiah 29:11.

CHAPTER FOUR: DO YOU KNOW I AM WORN OUT?
HE DOES NOT GROW WEARY.

1. P. L. Tan, *Encyclopedia of 7700 Illustrations: A Treasury of Illustrations, Anecdotes, Facts and Quotations for Pastors, Teachers and Christian Workers* (Garland, Texas: Bible Communications, 1996).
2. See Isaiah 40:28; Psalm 121; Jeremiah 31:25; Isaiah 40:31; Mark 6:31; Matthew 11:28–30; Exodus 20.

CHAPTER FIVE: DO YOU KNOW I AM SUFFERING WITH A THORN?
HE IS MY SUFFICIENCY.

1. Smith, *The God of All Comfort*, 192.
2. See 2 Corinthians 12:9; Philippians 4:19; 2 Corinthians 9:8; Jeremiah 32:17; Psalm 24:8; 147:5; 62:11; Romans 4:21; Mark 10:27.

CHAPTER SIX: DO YOU KNOW I AM A SINNER? HE IS MY SAVIOR.

1. See Titus 2:10; Romans 3:23; 5:8; John 3:16–17; Matthew 1:21; 1 John 1:9; Hebrews 10:22; Jude 24; 1 Corinthians 10:13; Romans 6:4, 11, 14; 8:35, 31.

CHAPTER SEVEN: DO YOU KNOW I AM LONELY? HE IS HERE.

1. Source: Bible.org.
2. Tim Hansel, *Through the Wilderness of Loneliness* (Elgin, Ill.: David C. Cook, 1991), 59–60.
3. H. W. Smith and M. E. Dieter, *The Christian's Secret of a Holy Life: The Unpublished Personal Writings of Hannah Whitall Smith* (Oak Harbor, Wash.: Logos Research Systems, Inc., 1997).
4. See Psalm 139:7–8; 142:4; 116:1; Acts 17:27; Hebrews 11:13–16; 1 Thessalonians 4:17; Psalm 34:18; 116:5; Isaiah 61:3; 51:10–12; Psalm 91:1–2; Lamentations 3:22–26.

CHAPTER EIGHT: DO YOU KNOW I AM UNDISCIPLINED?
HE IS MY STRENGTH.

1. http://www.angelfire.com/wi3/boppananny/In_Chambers__May_4.wps.htm.

2. R. H. Mounce, *Romans* (electronic ed.), Logos Library System; Vol. 27: The New American Commentary (168) (Nashville: Broadman & Holman Publishers, 1995, 2001).
3. John MacArthur, *The Pillars of Christian Character* (Wheaton, Ill.: Crossway, 1998). Subjects headings are from MacArthur; text under each is mine.
4. P. L. Tan, *Encyclopedia of 7700 Illustrations: A Treasury of Illustrations, Anecdotes, Facts and Quotations for Pastors, Teachers and Christian Workers* (Garland, Tex.: Bible Communications, 1979, 1996).
5. See Psalm 118:14; Isaiah 12:2; Psalm 93:1; 121; Proverbs 24:5; 31:25; Zechariah 4:6; Psalm 18:32; Isaiah 40:29; 30:15; 40:30; Nehemiah 8:10; Proverbs 24:5; Ephesians 6:11; Philippians 4:13.

CHAPTER NINE: DO YOU KNOW I AM GUARDED? HE IS GENEROUS.

1. See John 3:16; Ephesians 5:1; John 10:10; Luke 6:38; James 1:17; Luke 6:28; 1 Peter 4:8; 2 Corinthians 9:6–9; James 1:27; Romans 12:13.

CHAPTER TEN: DO YOU KNOW I AM ORDINARY? HE IS MY KING AND I AM HIS DAUGHTER.

1. See John 1:12–13; Romans 8:15–17; 1:7; John 17:9; Psalm 45:10–15; 1 Peter 2:9; John 17:23; Ephesians 3:17–19; Romans 8:38–39; 2 Corinthians 1:20.

CHAPTER ELEVEN: DO YOU KNOW I AM BROKEN?
HE IS MY REDEEMER.

1. We ended up titling that book *My Single Mom Life*. It is the full-volume set of my kung pao single mom life, only with a more vanilla title so people would get it.
2. See Romans 3:24; 8:30, 33; Psalm 147:3; Philippians 2:7–8; Ruth 2:11–12.

CHAPTER TWELVE: DO YOU KNOW I AM DISAPPOINTED? HE IS MY HOPE.

1. Mike Feazell, "Lessons on Mark: A Lesson on Hope," © 2005, www.christianodyssey.com.
2. See Psalm 65:5; 9:18; 43:5; 119:81; Titus 1:1–2; Psalm 130:7; 1 Peter 1:3; Jeremiah 17:7–8; Numbers 23:19; Jeremiah 17:7; Romans 5:5; Ephesians 1:18; Hebrews 11:1; 10:23; 6:19.

ACKNOWLEDGMENTS

T his book has been a journey with lots of turns, so there are many to thank.

Thanks to Jessica Wolstenholm and Kathy Helmers for the title. I believe you heard from God. Thanks also to the rest of the team at Creative Trust—Dan Raines, Jeanne Kaserman, and Jim Houser. Your years of support and management have been an incredible blessing to my family and me. May God multiply back to you all that you have given.

Thanks to my manager and friend, David Huffman, and his amazing wife, Amy. We will look toward the future together with great anticipation. It is a privilege to call you brother on this journey.

Thank you to my publisher, Jonathan Merkh, and editor, Philis Boulinghouse, at Howard, Simon & Schuster. What a privilege to work together. Cheryl Dunlop has been so great to edit, give insights, and make this manuscript stronger. Thanks, Cheryl.

My friends at the Extraordinary Women conferences have cheered me on and prayed me through this writing. Many, many thanks to Julie Clinton, Beth Cleveland, Jimmy Queen, Karen Kingsbury, Candace Cameron Bure, Stormie Omartian, Michelle McKinney Hammond, Chonda Pierce, Lisa Priscock, and Will

Montgomery. Seeing my EW family every weekend has become such a sweet place of rest and encouragement. I love you all.

Thank you to all the ladies who attend the conferences where I speak. Thank you for reading my books, doing the DVD Bible studies, standing in line to tell me your stories, and writing sweet notes on Facebook. I love my work with all my heart, but your encouragement gives me fresh energy and renewed passion. So thank you very, very much.

For the last ten years, Lisa Stridde has taken care of my travel details, merchandise shipping, and more filing than it seems like one speaker girl should have. But more important, Lisa has walked this journey alongside me as faithful friend. Thank you, Lisa, for every encouragement you have given to me. You serve with such grace and diligence. May God richly bless your family and your life because you live to honor Him by giving.

Thank you to Laura Johnson. I hope the years to come mean more time together.

Thanks to Scott Lindsey and Logos Bible Software. You are all amazing and brilliant! Your work has completely restructured my studies. I now spend entirely too much time reading *just one more* commentary, but I love that you have given me limitless options. And on my iPhone too. Thanks my friend.

A very special thank you to Jerry and Carlye Arnold. Your Texas love is big and your hearts so gracious and good. I love, love you.

Thank you to my new friend Denise Tolton, the Director of Women's Ministries at Westover Church in Greensboro, North Carolina. Our connection was so immediate and good. Thank you for every encouragement and prayer. I can't wait to know you more.

A year and a half ago, I was married and my family doubled. I couldn't be happier about all the people God has given me to love. Thank you to my parents, Joe and Novie Thomas. Your love is so consistent and strong. And to my new parents, Walt and Faye Pharr, thank you for loving me as your own. Thank you to my brothers and their families, JT, Jodi, Cole, and Craig. My new brother and his family, Walter, AnnaDell, William, Davidson, and

Molly Claire. I love you all. May we laugh together and love one another with grace and strength in all our days.

Thank you to the coolest kids on earth, Taylor, Grayson, William, and AnnaGrace. We've had a big year and you've cheered me through another round of writing. Thank you for every hug and snuggle and "Go Mom" you have given. I am so proud to belong to you.

My precious husband, Scott. Right this very minute, I am finishing up this book and you have gone to Sears to buy a dryer replacement thingamajig gadget. This is after working all day, picking up the kids from basketball and dance, and then stopping to get takeout for the deadline mama. I have never, ever known someone who gives so purely and freely. Your consistent happiness is amazing to me. Your love and attention are what I had only hoped marriage could be, but never expected to experience on this earth. I have made two really great decisions in my lifetime. One, asking Jesus to be my Savior. Two, marrying you. Thank you for making this life brighter and sweeter. Thank you for praying over me every night. Thank you for protecting me and making me safe. Thank you for loving my children as your own. Thank you becoming a family of six without a blink or hesitation. Thank you for loving my job and standing at the back so proud. Thank you for coffee in the morning and walking the dogs before I get up. I pray I can give to you with the lavish measure you give to me. They say a great marriage is when each one believes they got the better deal. I am sure I got the better deal. We are so very blessed.

And my Jesus, all my praise belongs to You. Thank You for knowing me truly and loving me still. Thank You for every gift of love You have given to me. Thank You for the ministry You have given to me. Thank You for the promise of eternity and the power of Your presence on this earth. With everything I have, may You be honored and glorified. May this book and these words point every reader to You. Not to me, oh Lord, but to You be the glory.

ABOUT THE AUTHOR

Angela Thomas is a popular national speaker and the bestselling author of ten books and Bible studies, including *Do You Think I'm Beautiful?* She is a graduate of the University of North Carolina and Dallas Theological Seminary and has been teaching the Bible for more than twenty-five years, using her unique gifts of entertaining storytelling and faithful biblical instruction. Every year she speaks to thousands of women across the United States and around the world. Angela and her family make their home in North Carolina.

INTRODUCTION

In her book *Do You Know Who I Am?* Angela Thomas asks God if He knows her—and ultimately does He love her—as she is, right now, today. In each chapter, she names a different identity issue, such as: "I am invisible," "I am worn out," "I am undisciplined," "I am ordinary," and "I am afraid to dream." With each honest admission, Angela teaches that God lovingly replies, "Yes, I know your heart. I see your struggle. Now . . . do you know who I AM?"

Ultimately Angela reveals that the answer to being known and loved lies in an intimate understanding of who God is. Each identity struggle is answered with a short biblical study on the character of God that assures readers that their personal, spiritual, and eternal fulfillment is not dependent on getting themselves together. Rather, God has a purpose for them just as they are broken, afraid, disappointed, disillusioned.

Through vivid storytelling, biblical teaching, and practical application, readers will find the heartfelt answers they seek.

DISCUSSION QUESTIONS

1. Angela writes that her friend and housecleaner, Beverly, was great spiritual support in her life, and may even have been an angel. Have you encountered such a person in your life? How can you be a "Beverly" to someone else?

2. Is there a big dream that you've been putting off pursuing for any reason? What is it, and why haven't you been pursuing it? How are you investing your talents? Are you "living worthy"?

3. As you seek comfort from God in your own life, remember to also ask him who you can give comfort to. Pray for a friend in need.

4. In Chapter Four, Angela lists lessons that have been ministered to her about how God helps those who are weary. His presence restores, waiting often restores, the Sabbath restores, repent, have Godly, refreshing friends, etc. Think about other lessons God may have shown you, and share them with your group.

5. What is your "thorn"? What could God be showing you by not removing it right now? How can you use your weaknesses to be a stronger person, and strengthen your faith?

6. Think back to how you felt when you first accepted God into your life. Is there a sin you've committed since then that you've been rationalizing or neglecting to realize the importance of? If so, this is your wakeup call—make a conscious choice to Run Away! Turn to God and your book group to help.

7. Pray the prayer on page 141, that God will comfort you in times of loneliness. Then pray for someone else who may need God's support more than you.

8. Angela struggles with diet and exercise, which is common among many women. What is your struggle? Where do you desire discipline in your life? Share with your group, and help to hold each other accountable.

9. Are you a "cheerful giver"? Think of everyday ways that you can be a more generous reflection of God. Then let your book group know a little something extra you did this week, and how it made you feel. Inspire each other!

10. Angela writes about Satan preying on your weak places and holding you back. First, think about your true strengths and talents. Ask yourself, where do you need to keep a door open for God? What do you need to let go of?

11. Everyone has suffered disappointment and loss in their lives. Think about a trying circumstance in your life. How has it shaped you into the person you are today? Have you allowed tragedy to change you for the better?

12. Make a list of your struggles, needs, weak places and insecurities. Be honest with yourself and with each other, and offer them up to God together. How has reading Do You Know Who I Am? helped you face and overcome the obstacles in your life?

13. Which chapter do you relate to the most? Why? Share with your group. How can you help support each other with your different struggles?

ENHANCE

1. If you'd like to hear more from Angela Thomas, consider attending one of her speaking engagements. Check out www.AngelaThomas.com to find one near you!
2. Read one of the books Angela recommends in the Introduction, such as *Knowing God* by J.I. Packer, *The God of All Comfort* by Hannah Whitall Smith, *The Knowledge of the Holy* by A.W. Towzer, or *Your God Is Too Small* by J.B. Phillips. How do they enhance or influence the message of *Do You Know Who I Am?*
3. Angela writes about learning many life lessons at her family's fruit stand. As you were growing up, was there a place or experience, outside school, that helped to shape your life?
4. In Chapter Nine, Angela extols the virtues of working hard. She writes, "Physical labor clears your head and gives you immediate accomplishment rewards," (p. 191). Spend a day working hard, either volunteering, helping a neighbor, or in your own garden.

AUTHOR Q&A

You write that you originally had many more chapter ideas, and that you whittled them down to these twelve. Why did you pick these? What were some others you considered?

Well, since you ask, a few of the other ideas were:

I am in over my head.	I am nothing special.
I am co-dependent.	I am fragile.
I am ashamed.	I am insecure.
I am angry.	I am tempted.
I am confused.	I am a doubter.
I am judgmental.	I am lazy.
I am proud.	I am addicted.
I am pretending.	I am unmotivated.
I am indifferent.	I am playing it safe.
I am stubborn.	I am rebellious.
I am a gossip.	I am bitter.
I am hurt.	I am sad.
I am depressed.	I am discouraged.
I am a failure.	I am apathetic.
I am defeated.	I am anxious.
I am impatient.	

So many of these thoughts overlap in some way. And there was no way to do each idea justice. So I pared them down into groups and tried to shoot for the bigger ideas and struggles that might be more common to every woman.

You mention that you travel a lot with your work. Where is your favorite, most memorable place to visit, and why?

Outside of the United States, I have traveled to South Africa four times. I love the people and their passion so much. Their beautiful country takes my breath away and the powerful presence of God has given me experiences unlike any I have ever known. Visit www.beautyforashes.co.za to learn more about women's ministry in that country.

Through World Vision, my family also sponsors four children who live in South Africa. I had the amazing opportunity to visit them a couple of years ago. They completely stole my heart and I cannot help but think of them often, pray for their safety and hope for the day I'll see them again. If you'd like to sponsor a child anywhere in this world, please go to www.worldvision.org. I have seen the work they are doing with my own eyes. Lives and families and villages are being changed for good because World Vision is present and working where the rest of us aren't able to go. God willing, one day we will sponsor an entire tribe. The need is so great.

Traveling inside the US, I am a North Carolina girl through and through. But I do have to tell you that I smile when I see Texas on my schedule. I think it has something to do with the guacamole and the really cool people who live there.

How did you discover what God's calling was in your life? What is your advice to those who are still searching for theirs?

In 1984, after college, I was at home working for my dad full time and volunteering with the student ministry at my church. I truly cared about my dad's business and the opportunities that were waiting for me there, but over the course of 8 or 9 months, my heart for those students could not be ignored. All I could think about was how to help them. What could I do to reach them with the truths of Jesus? How could I make the Bible come alive for them? Clear as day, I knew that knowing the Bible and correctly applying it's truth meant more to me than anything. I believe with all of my heart that I was called by God. What is interesting is that the call has never wavered. I have known everyday of the past 26 years what I was put on this earth to do. How and where and when have all been big questions. But the what has never changed – Angela, just teach the word of God. I think that is one of the sweetest gifts I have received from God.

At many moments in the book, you recount things that were going on in your life as you were writing. It really feels like the reader was with you every step of the way. How long did it actually take you to write this book?

The book probably took about a year to come together. And in the editing process I was able to add updates and a few more personal stories. I know that I writing about dieting to fit into my wedding dress and in just a couple months I will have been married two years. Maybe that helps to give a timeframe to the writing. The stories seem like they happen one after another, but believe me, there is a lot of carpooling and homework and laundry in between!

I'm sure readers are wondering how things turned out after your cancer scare; can you share with us how you're doing now?

Thanks for asking. My mom has had ovarian cancer, so my gynecologist is on high alert with regard to cancer for me. I am still seeing him about every three months. He says that my cervical tests are not perfect, but they are no longer pre-cancerous. With regard to ovarian cancer because of my mom's diagnosis, I take a blood test called CA-125 and have an ultra-sound every six months. Ugh. Why can't this be the kind of concern where they need to look in your ear?

Was it hard to select so many perfectly appropriate Bible verses throughout the book? You quote from more than one version of the Bible; do you have a favorite?

I teach from the NIV, mostly. I used to study from the NASB, and still love it, but I have landed with the NIV as my go-to translation. I love THE MESSAGE in small doses, especially to make a familiar passage seem brand new to the listener. I also have the coolest Bible software called LOGOS so that I am able to read every translation ever printed. Sometimes that's overkill, but I am such a nerd that I love it!!

How do your children and husband feel about you sharing personal details and humorous stories about them?

My kids have grown up with the stories. And bless them, they know that our stories really do help people to understand more about God. My husband married into the story-telling and knew what he was getting before he ever decided to propose. For my part, I would never tell a story that is embarrassing for them or cutting or wounding. I will never break their confidence or tell something they have asked me not to share. We have had a few conversations that began, "Mom, you can't put this in a book." Smile. They know me pretty well.

You mention that you've overcome obstacles in your past, such as divorce, and that you have not been invited to speak to certain audiences because of it. Do you agree with that decision? How has your past influenced your ministry?

I have learned to let God open the doors and take me where He wants me to be. That's so much easier than acting like I ought to be invited anywhere. Married, single, divorced, remarried, I promise you that what I get to do is one of the greatest privileges this life can hold. I do not take it lightly that God uses me anywhere and anyway He sees fit. I am honored and humbled. And time is such a beautiful teacher for all of us. There have been people who said, "I'm sorry we can't invite you," and then years later, changed their minds. God is the Redeemer. I am trusting Him with how He chooses to minister through my brokenness.

Truth is, God has given me more work to do than there are weekends in my year. I am blessed beyond measure. And even if the phone stops ringing tomorrow, and no one invites me anywhere, anymore, I'll still open the Bible and ask some people to come for coffee and tell them everything I can about the amazing truths of God.

This book is written specifically towards women. How do you think the same ideas might apply to men as well?

Honestly, I'm not sure the struggles are the same. My husband has been so gracious to listen to me mull over these ideas, but I know that many of the weak places in me are completely different for him. Ultimately, every truth about the character of God that you read in this book is intended for men and women, boys and girls, young and old. That is one of the coolest things about teaching the Word of God, I may be talking to women, but they can go home and tell the man they love, or the child they raise, a brand new truth from God's Word and the power of truth to change their life is the same.

You write in your introduction that you were originally trying to write another book when you were overcome with the idea for this one. What was that first book about? Are you finishing it now? If not, what are you working on currently?

I think I have shelved the other book and in the end, incorporated some of its strongest ideas into this one. Right now I am working on a DVD curriculum and a devotional. I have an idea for the next book, but I guess I ought to call my editor before I spill the beans.

please visit
AngelaThomas.com

If you would like to schedule
Angela for an engagement
in your community,
visit AngelaThomas.com and go
to the speaking section or email:
atscheduling@brandWAVESLLC.com

join the Angela
Thomas community
on facebook

Available February 1, 2011...

BRAVE

Honest Questions
Women Ask

**A small-group Bible study resource DVD and study from
Angela Thomas dealing with the subjects in "Do You Know
Who I Am?"**

**If you want to dig deeper into the truths from this book
with friends such as small group or church and see Angela's
video teaching then check out BRAVE, coming in February
2011.**